ANTONI GAUDÍ

1   Gaudí as a young man, ca. 1890

ANTONI GAUDÍ

Architecture in Barcelona

Author: Gabriele Sterner
Translator: Roger Marcink

BARRON'S

Woodbury, New York / London / Toronto / Sydney

Front cover illustration: Roof walkway with chimneys, Casa Milá, Barcelona
Back cover illustration: Barcelona city map showing location of Gaudí's
   buildings

First edition © Copyright 1979, DuMont Book Publishers, Cologne. All
   rights for all countries reserved by DuMont Buchverlag GmbH & Co.
   Kommanditgesellschaft, Cologne, West Germany. The title of the
   German edition is: Gabriele Sterner, *Barcelona, Antoni Gaudí.*

All inquiries should be addressed to:
Barron's Educational Series, Inc.
113 Crossways Park Drive
Woodbury, New York 11797

Library of Congress Catalog Card No. 82-6868
International Standard Book No. 0-8210-2293-9

Library of Congress Cataloging in Publication Data

Sterner, Gabriele, 1946–
   Antoni Gaudí—architecture in Barcelona.
   Translation of: Barcelona, Antoni Gaudí
   Bibliography: p. 162
   Includes index.
   1. Gaudí, Antoni, 1852–1926.   2. Architecture—Spain—Barce-
   lona.   I. Title.
NA1313.G3S7313 1982   720'.92'4   82-6868
ISBN 0-8120-2293-9   AACR2

PRINTED IN HONG KONG
5678   041   987654321

Contents

"Suffer my bold and daring approximations. And since neither idle curiosity nor foolish self-importance nor love for anything other than for You (God) inspires me with such thoughts, be my guardian and guide me on this path, as I am venturing into the labyrinth of the world of nature and trying to search for You in Your works. . . ."

Anthony Ashley Cooper (1671–1713), *The Moralists*

◁ 2 Gaudí in the Corpus Christi procession in Barcelona, 1924

Introduction

Nature and Geometry

"Originality is achieved by returning to origins." This remark of Gaudí's contains the maxim central to his creative activity, for what he worked toward was the fusion of nature and geometry, which he regarded as the two roots of all things.

The perfect unity of form and structure which Gaudí achieved gives his work a special place in the history of architecture. In his buildings, structure *is* form, and texture assumes an organic role in the structure. Architectonically, their mode of construction remains geometric and subject to geometric laws. But it is unusual, indeed, even prophetic, in the sense that Gaudí's "geometry" combines the straight lines of his façades with parabolic and hyperbolic curves. These are geometric forms that derive from nature, from natural growth, and not from artificial abstraction. The masonry work of Gaudí's buildings is self-sufficient, so to speak, consisting of self-contained units that require no additional supports or props. The quality of equilibrium, which Eugene Viollet-le-Duc attributed to the architectonic works of the Gothic period in his article "Design," had normative value for Gaudí. But, in Gaudí's eyes, the "equilibrium" of the Gothic cathedrals was specious: without their buttresses, they would collapse. Gaudí therefore called Gothic architecture "incomplete" and "industrial." His own works, however, he frequently described as "Grecian." In terms of their external form this may seem absurd, yet the contrapposto of a classic Greek statue represents precisely the kind of "equilibrium" Gaudí sought to attain. But Gaudí found the most striking examples of his ideal of equilibrium in nature.

"You want to know where I found my model?" Gaudí answered his own question by pointing to a eucalyptus tree in front of his studio window: "A tree bears its branches, and they in turn bear the twigs, and they the leaves. And each individual part grows harmoniously, beautifully, since the artist God Himself created the whole. This tree needs no external help. All its parts are balanced in themselves. Everything in it is in equilibrium."

This is the outstanding characteristic of Gaudí's architecture, too, in which we find parabolic arches; mushroom-shaped capitals; fragile, hanging vaults without visible lateral thrusts; interior columns. "Have you ever observed that a cane bends under the weight of the person using it? In a similar way, my columns are stone canes in which, as we can easily see, the principle of supports and loads is embodied."

Gaudí's architecture was based on a subtle intellectual edifice that we can best reconstruct by studying the works themselves. Analysis of the design and structure of individual buildings will provide the key to an understanding of his work. Gaudí's greatness lay in his ability to combine architecture and intellectual content in tangible, unified form. He conceived his buildings in an almost visionary way, yet it would be a mistake to separate conception and execution. The most appropriate and critical approach to his work, then, is not to fit it into any preconceived theory but rather to let intellectual content reveal itself in the completed building. Nevertheless, by way of introduction and as an aid to a better understanding of his work, I will mention a few of his major theses here.

Gaudí's esthetic system arose from a process of ongoing inspiration. Innovations to which he gave concrete architectural shape spawned new ideas and concepts. His ideas were a kind of commentary on what he had already created; and as he moved ahead in his work, one esthetic idea would be overlaid by another that had emerged from it. Gaudí's theory and practice thus remained in a state of constant flux in which new ideas cancelled out and replaced the old ideas from which they had emerged.

Beauty

Early in his career Gaudí set out to comprehend the principle of "beauty"; and in the course of his studies, he came to the conclusion that an object could be called beautiful if its form was functional, free from superfluities, and in harmony with its material. The product had

9

to be heterogeneous and the character of the work visible. The character of a work lay, he said, in "the definition of its esthetic and moral conditions." The exterior had to be a mirror, as it were, of the interior, i.e., a mirror of the building's function. Public buildings, for example, should be reserved in character; geometric ornamentation, set off by contrasting natural forms, is appropriate for them. Churches should be grand in their proportions, sparsely ornamented, and unified in form. The ornamentation should follow as a logical consequence of the structure, the material, and the economic determinants.

Proportion and Color

Closely related to the design and character of a building is the question of its "proportions." For Gaudí, proportion meant the mutual harmony of the individual parts among themselves, of the whole in relation to the individual parts, and of the individual parts in relation to the whole. In this connection, Gaudí mentions the necessary detailed study of natural forms, which has to be considered in terms of the technical possibilities available to the architect at his time in history. The results of this study also have to be adapted to the demands of the site in order to produce a satisfactory solution—a solution, in other words, that sees the esthetic factors of an object in terms of the mechanical peculiarities of the materials used. Gaudí viewed the problem of color from a similar perspective. Natural forms never present themselves to us monochromatically. It therefore seemed necessary to him to completely or partially color architectonic elements. At the same time, color emphasizes the significance of the individual parts, makes them appear more elegant, and highlights their functions. For Gaudí, elegance resulted from the proper elicitation of beauty. Elegance is beauty achieved by minimal means, that is, beauty embodied in clear and simplified forms.

The "Truth"

Just as elegance and beauty were inseparable for Gaudí, beauty and truth were identical for him, too. Beauty was the manifestation of truth; or, to put it more clearly: without truth there could be no beauty. The
10

artist's fundamental task was to create "beautiful works that are not motivated by expectations of profit." It is permissible and even necessary for a businessman to be guided by material considerations, but an artist must disregard everything that diverts him from the path of beauty. The high moral standard underlying all of Gaudí's work is evident in this principle.

Beauty is truth, but it is life as well, and life is manifest in the creation. While man may be the most perfect work in the creation, Gaudí did not think man himself was capable of creation. Man merely makes discoveries and builds on those discoveries. The artist has to imbue his work with life. He accomplishes this with movement and color; however, he must not succumb to the temptation to arouse emotions that are not genuine. Feelings lacking in truth, feelings evoked by mere tricks and not originating from insight into nature, were anathema to Gaudí.

Profound study is necessary if one is to find the truth, study that makes use of both analysis and synthesis. Analysis, however, which considers only the individual parts, has to be subordinated to synthesis, which embraces the whole and which yields the unity essential to any work of art. For Gaudí, to create meant to unify, to set parts in relation to one another, not to separate them. Gaudí's goal was to bring together highly diverse elements into a harmonious whole, making them serve a single idea of a nearly visionary nature.

Gaudí's ideas were exacting and often difficult to realize in practice, but they are clearly evident in the major works we will discuss in the following chapters. Gaudí chose means of expression appropriate to his ideas and incorporated their specific qualities into his overall conception.

The Catalan Environment and the Neo-Gothic Style

Gaudí was, as were most young Catalans of his generation, a passionate nationalist. Shortly after his graduation from the Escola Superior, he joined the Centre Excursionista—a group of young men organized by Catalan nationalists to make trips to such shrines of patriotic pride and medieval grandeur as Montserrat, Elne, Majorca, Pic della Maladeta, and Toulouse. At the same time, Gaudí was intensely concerned with social problems and studied French writings relevant to this interest. In the Societat Obrera Mataronese, he came together with the organizers of the cooperative movement in Catalonia. Gaudí's first attempt at city planning envisioned a complex including workers' housing, a factory, and social facilities. The concept was based on the cooperative idea and may have been influenced by Fourier or even by the Englishman Owens. The plans for this project were exhibited at the Paris Exposition in 1878.

Gaudí was a Spaniard but, even more so, a Catalan.

> The Catalans are neither French nor Spanish. They are a nation of their own not only in language and dress but in their way of life as well. Their impetuosity and their enterprising spirit leave no doubt in the traveller's mind that he is no longer in refined, carefree Spain. . . . Children of the Celtiberians, they are striving for their previous independence; their patriotism is highly local and centers around their own village church. Catalonia, with its Cleons in calico and its Catalan women in cotton, is both the strong and weak link of Spain, and no province of the disjointed entity making up the official kingdom "de las Españas" is less in touch with the crown than this classic land of revolt, which is always on the verge of secession. (Richard Ford, *A Handbook for Travellers in Spain and Readers at Home*. London: J. Murray, 1845.)

Catalonia's relationship to Spain, like Ireland's to England, has always been problematic; but the great difference is that Catalonia is the principal industrial area of the peninsula and not an underdeveloped, impoverished region. Spanish unity had always been threatened by the Catalans, who were more drawn to their Provençal neighbors than to their own countrymen and who had always forcefully asserted their free, enlightened spirit. Linguistically and culturally, Catalonia was more an offshoot of France than a part of Spain. In 1876, after the defeat of the Carlists, who were the supporters of the pretender to the crown Don Carlos de Bourbon, Catalan nationalism developed into a revolutionary movement. In the years 1822 to 1837 Catalonia had lost its penal code, its commercial law, its right to mint money, its special courts, and even its right to use the Catalan language in its schools. These restrictions strengthened the left wing of the nationalist party, which, although weak numerically, was influential, since most of the intellectuals belonged to it. This intellectual elite propagated the revival and reintroduction of medieval traditions in Catalan literature and architecture.

The Middle Ages represented the high point of Catalan independence

12

and prosperity to which the Catalans yearned to return. In the thirteenth and fourteenth centuries, Barcelona controlled trade in the western Mediterranean. Its commercial domain extended as far as Naples, Sicily and Greece. The discovery of America and the destruction of Mediterranean trade by the Turks brought a decline in Barcelona's commercial importance and, hence, in its political influence. The resurgence of affluence that followed industrial development in the nineteenth century prompted a desire for a renaissance of the past era.

The Gothic style thus represented Catalan national and economic independence. It flourished when Barcelona achieved economic importance, and it was considered a native style, as opposed to the Mozarabic architecture of the conquered Moors. The architectural style of the French cathedral had taken hold in Catalonia by the end of the twelfth century. Characteristic features that often appear in Catalan cathedrals are the vast width and height of the nave and side aisles, the entry halls, and the use of buttresses between which side-aisle chapels were placed. The nave of the cathedral in Palma de Mallorca, for example, is 42.5 meters [139.4 feet] high and 19.5 meters [64 feet] wide. The pillars are nearly 24.5 meters [80.4 feet] high and make those of Amiens, which are 14.65 meters [48 feet] high, seem small in comparison.

Many Catalan architects — heeding Viollet le Duc's plea not just to imitate but to carry on the Gothic tradition—built churches in the style of Catalonia's "golden age." When Villar, the architect for El Temple de la Sagrada Familia [Church of the Holy Family] resigned his post, Martorell, an advocate of the neo-Gothic, recommended the thirty-one-year-old Antoni Gaudí to replace him.

Some of the most important artists of the twentieth century have come from Catalonia, and they all follow in the tradition of their country. Pablo Picasso, one of the most restless artists of our century, destroyer and pioneer in one, represents the dissonant vein in Spanish art. The work of Juan Gris, who brought Cubism to classic perfection, displays a restraint comparable to that of Zurbaran; Miró's surreal world of fable draws on the tradition of Romanesque painting; Salvador Dali is a speculative verist who often resorts to illusion. Prominent among the younger painters is the stark nihilist Antonio Tapies. Catalan ironwork, the tradition of which reaches back to the Gothic period, provided the inspiration for Julio Gonzalez, the founder of modern ironwork sculpture, and, more recently, for Eduardo Chillida. And the current turn toward plastic form that architecture is taking obliges us to recognize Gaudí as a precursor of this trend in contemporary architecture.

Mediterraneanism

Just as Gaudí's style was a confirmation of Catalonia's new patriotism and self-awareness, so his personal being was an expression of these same feelings. Gaudí was as much at one with the Mediterranean as his Catalan homeland was.

For Gaudí, the essentials of beauty were harmony and color, and in his opinion these qualities could develop to a far greater extent in the temperate regions of our world than in areas of climatic extremes.

The inhabitants of the countries on the Mediterranean feel beauty with a greater intensity than people in equatorial or northern countries can, and they are quite conscious of this. The most remarkable art works throughout history have been created by Mediterranean artists, that is, by Egyptians, Greeks, Italians, and Spaniards. The reason for this is that they have a more strongly rooted concept of beauty, and this in turn derives from their proximity to the benign Mediterranean and from the position of the sun in their sky. Mediterranean sunlight, falling at an angle of 45 degrees, provides ideal conditions for observing nature and the elements.

The Mediterraneanism that Gaudí celebrated and practiced did not, however, make him blind to artistic innovations in the rest of Europe. Thus, he drew inspiration from early Art Nouveau, anticipated some of its essential developments, and carried them to a perfection all his own.

In the equatorial and polar regions of the earth, people are compelled, as it were, to see things "incorrectly." They suffer either from an almost intolerable excess of light or from a lack of it. As a result, images cannot have a "natural" appearance for them but take on fantastic qualities instead. This is why people living in extreme regions develop an overwrought fantasy and, at the same time, a heightened capacity for abstraction, qualities which then manifest themselves in the art, literature, philosophy, and other disciplines cultivated in these regions.

The optimal light and climate of the temperate zones allow a more

14

realistic view of things, and the inhabitants of these zones enjoy such a perception of the world almost as their birthright. They have a more highly developed creative imagination, because their creativity is based on reality, which is to say, on truth.

Gaudí distinguishes carefully between fantasy, which arises from a distorted sense of reality, and the creative imagination, which is based on real images. For him, these are irreconcilable opposites. Those who call Gaudí's work "fantastic" are misusing his own terminology, and it is equally erroneous to seek the roots of Gaudí's art in non-Mediterranean countries. His inspiration is indissolubly connected with the Mediterranean and its sunny coasts.

"Let us think," he liked to say, "what it means to be born near the Mediterranean. It means that we are as far removed from the dazzling light of the tropics as we are from the specter-producing darkness of the north. We are brothers to the Italians, and that makes us more able sculptors. . . . Catalans have a natural sense of plasticity that gives them a conception of things as a whole and of the relationship of things among themselves. The sea and the light of the Mediterranean countries generate this admirable clarity, and this is why the things of reality never mislead the Mediterranean people but instruct them instead."

Life and Background

Gaudí's life and work form an indissoluble unity. Just as the individual elements of his buildings blended together into a harmonious whole, so his personal life was at one with his professional activity. Both were guided by the principles of sacrifice and renunciation.

Gaudí had a strong, passionate temperament that his keen intellect sought to control. However, both in his life and in his art, what appeared to be irreconcilable opposites worked together to yield a "balanced dynamic." A capacity for enthusiasm presupposes intellect in addition to emotion. Feeling, contemplation, and powers of imagination and conceptualization all working in concert cannot produce mere mediocrity. Gaudí's buildings were not conceived in accordance with any routine scheme in which prescribed answers are given to prescribed questions. They emerged instead as a reaction to experience and to life, i.e., to the relationship between beauty and necessity. A work of art expresses the individuality of the person who has created it. The variety of the person's experiences, inner conflicts, and relationship with the outside world will be recorded with it. Gaudí's father was a coppersmith. His earlier ancestors were potters. Hence his ability to conceptualize his works in three dimensions and to work out the solutions to his construction problems in the round, and not on the drafting table. From his grandfather, who was a potter, Gaudí inherited the capacity to visualize his work three-dimensionally. From his father, the coppersmith, he inherited the craftsman's feel and instinct for his medium. Working from this double legacy, Gaudí created buildings that interact with the space they occupy and that reveal undisguised the static forces at play in them.

Tarragona, which is near Reus, Gaudí's place of birth, is known for its beautiful buildings. Good architecture was a tradition in the region, and there is no doubt that Gaudí was influenced by the surroundings in which he grew up. The stone and brick construction used there left its mark on his work, and he drew inspiration from the remains of Roman aqueducts and temples as well as from the early Gothic cathedral of Tarragona. The rhythm of the façade of the Casa Milá or of the serpentine bench in Park Güell can be seen both in the classical gable friezes and in the mountain silhouettes of Catalonia.

Religion and Politics

Gaudí's deep religiousness would seem to be at odds with his political and social commitment. But Catholicism as he lived it should not be mistaken for dogmatic sectarianism or false piety. Gaudí's striving for perfection, clarity, truth, and beauty inevitably led him closer to God. The creator of all things and of all life was what he sought. The voluntary asceticism of his last decades and his renunciation of worldly goods were the logical consequences of his religious thought. The shed at the building site of the Sagrada Familia was not just where Gaudí chose to live but his true home as well. Gaudí's social activism was not motivated by any political programs; it derived instead from his belief in the dignity of man and in the dignity of his nation. This belief gave him his keen sense of the practical and of human needs. His structures are always as functional as they are expressive. Gaudí never created art for art's sake as some of his critics claimed. His furniture, houses, and gardens always fulfill a real function.

16

Buildings and Residences Worthy of Man

Gaudí remains essentially an architect of the nineteenth century. Some of the stylistic means he used in realizing his progressive ideas are outmoded now, and he has consequently been labeled an "outsider" and a "fantast" by an art criticism that looks to functionalism as a panacea. It was right and necessary that a period of purism followed on the jumble of styles that dominated in the last century, but zeal for purity has blinded architects to the needs and demands of man. We have come to realize in recent years that man—who is part of nature—suffers adverse effects from living in the monotonous cubes of our big city housing developments. Only gradually are we returning to concepts such as "biological living" and the need to adapt a structure to its environment and to the requirements of its occupants. For Gaudí these considerations had top priority. He chose his building materials to suit the climatic conditions, and he used natural methods of ventilation that made it unnecessary to even open a window. Our debilitating air conditioners are a very poor substitute indeed. Anyone who has wandered through the endless halls of modern apartment houses yearns for short, well thought out corridors. Gaudí created living spaces with movable walls—a possibility we dream of but do not act on. Recent studies have shown that rectilinear spaces are at odds with what human beings naturally perceive to be a comfortable and secure living environment. The lines in Gaudí's interiors are curved. Garbage chutes, basement garages, and the incorporation of the outdoors were taken for granted in his designs. We must not let the original forms Gaudí developed mislead us as to his basic intent. In view of all this we can safely say that Gaudí was ahead of his time; and that with the help of reinforced concrete, he could have translated the ideas of his later years into structures compatible with our current sense of architectural style. We are in danger today of regarding architecture as an experiment remote from life and of letting technical means become ends in themselves. Gaudí's visionary power, his linking of the intellectual and the visual, not only can provide us with inspiration but can also show us the route we should take.

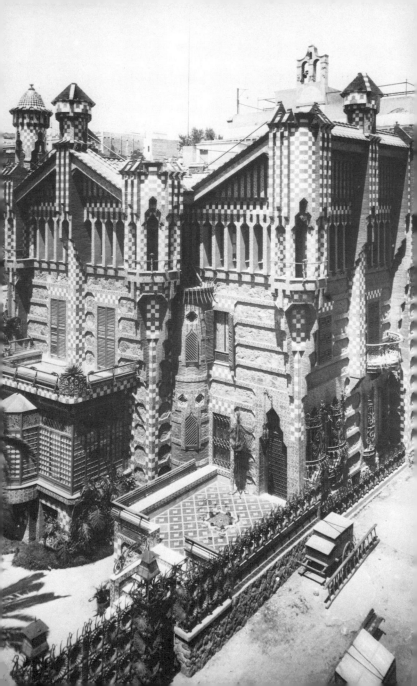

Casa Vicens, Barcelona
(Figs. 3–9)

Casa Vicens (Fig. 3) was built in 1883–1885 as a summer home for the tile dealer Manuel Vicens. This was the first commission Gaudí had received from a private individual. Until then, he had worked primarily on religious and public projects.

The Original Building

The construction site was in Gracia, a town that has since been incorporated into Barcelona. The relatively small plot of land at 24-26 Calle Carolinas was flanked by two walls, one of which belonged to a monastery. Gaudí used the available space to optimum advantage by placing the chalet-like house directly against the monastery wall. This astute arrangement left the garden in one undivided plot and made it appear quite large despite its small dimensions. An elliptical arch crowned with graceful brick arcades broke the massive lines of the wall on the other side of the lot. Luxuriant plantings and elaborate fountains created the impression of even greater space (Fig. 4). The brick wall of the monastery was covered with dense grape vines that gently framed the house.

The architecture of the building was clear and surveyable at a glance. The piers, braced by wooden crossbeams, ran parallel to the boundary wall; the interior load-bearing walls and the façade conformed to this same scheme. The gallery beams, also arranged horizontally, followed the gentle slope of the roof (Fig. 5).

The living rooms were on the ground floor and were entered by way of an atrium. The dining room was at the center of the house, sur-

◁ 3   Casa Vicens after the modifications of 1925

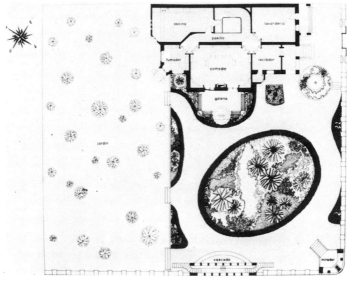

4 Casa Vicens. Original ground plan

5 Casa Vicens before 1925

6 Casa Vicens. Door leading to the garden from the small smoking room ▷

rounded by an enclosed gallery with unglazed windows, a smoking room (Fig. 7), and a drawing room. A spiral staircase led from the rear patio to the other floors, where the bedrooms were located. The basement contained the servants' quarters.

Casa Vicens Today

The basic layout of Casa Vicens was radically altered in 1925 when Dr. Antonio Jover acquired the property. Dr. Jover added a transom on the monastery side and made a number of other additions on the side of the house away from the street. With still further expansion in mind, he also purchased the lot adjoining the garden. The old church tower of Santa Rita stood on this lot, and when Dr. Jover expanded the garden to take in the neighboring lot, he incorporated this tower into his landscaping. All the changes were made under the supervision of the architect J. B. Serra, who respected the unique quality of Gaudí's work and sought Gaudí's advice on these changes. But despite this, the originality of this previously small building was destroyed. The spiral staircase was removed; the patio was converted to other uses; a fountain that had been located in front of an open, rectangular porch was torn down and the porch itself turned into a kind of winter garden. The present owner, Senore Jover de Herrera, assisted by the architect Antonio Pineda, is in the process of restoring the house to its original state.

At the beginning of his career—and this is the period in which he built Casa Vicens—Gaudí tried his hand in practically every historical style and experimented with a great variety of materials ranging from ceramic tiles to wrought iron. Like all his contemporaries, Gaudí was primarily interested in decorative elements, and it is therefore not surprising that the charm of Casa Vicens derives essentially from the lively textures of its beautifully conceived ornamentation. The basic material in the façade is an ocher-colored natural stone offset by unglazed brick, and the reddish tone of the brick contrasts in turn with the green, white, and yellow tile in the facing. Flowers and plants were painted on some of the tiles to make the masonry work blend in with the surrounding vines, which, unfortunately, have since been removed. The purpose of the ornamentation was not, however, to obscure function but rather to highlight it. Geometrical patterns embodied in rectilinear strips, brick-

7   Casa Vicens. Smoking room

8   Casa Vicens. Ventilation chimney ▷

work, and layers of stone drew attention to the arrangement of the stories. In the upper part of the building, the horizontal decoration is transmuted into vertical projections that stress the lines of the windows and flow upward to lend a deliberate emphasis to the chimneys. The varying patterns in the building are drawn together here in a checker-board motif executed in white and green tile (Fig. 8). This same motif recurs in the wrought iron fence and gate, too, where the square provides the setting for the palm-leaf pattern and represents the continuity inherent in nature (Fig. 9).

The vivid décor of the dining room sets the tone for the rest of the interior. The wall frescoes by the painter Torrecasana create a unified whole with a wooden-coffered ceiling decorated with floral patterns. The smoking room has a stalactite ceiling (Fig. 7). A small Renaissance fountain in the form of a baptismal font stood in the garden side of the previously unenclosed porch.

The obvious influence that Arabic art had on the Casa Vicens does not, however, take the form of mere "stylistic reminiscences." Gaudí was inspired by the same delight in ornamentation that had inspired the artists of the Orient.

◁ 9 Casa Vicens. Entrance gate

"El Capricho," Comillas near Santander (Fig. 10)

The country house in Comillas known as "El Capricho" was built in 1883–85 for Maximo Diaz de Quijano, and no satisfactory explanation has yet been offered as to how this small property acquired its unusual name.

The minaret-like tower and the small corner balconies apparently struck Gaudí's contemporaries as "capricious," and in the course of time this descriptive term took on the permanence of a proper name. The playful character of the building is evident, too, in its decorative details and in the richness of its colors (Fig. 10). Gaudí himself never went to Comillas, but he provided Cristobal Cascante, the local architect who supervised the construction of the house, with precise instructions. Gaudí never knew his client personally, either. Maximo Diaz de Quijano, a bachelor who had returned from the West Indies with a massive fortune, gave Gaudí a completely free hand in the design

In its overall conception and in many key details, "El Capricho" anticipates later developments in Gaudí's style. The plan is open and free. At its center is a winter garden; and, for all practical purposes, we could say that the rest of the house is built around this open core. The floor of this "glass room" is lower than the floor level in the rest of the house and opens onto a terrace enclosed by a wall. The villa is flooded with light because the main living room is illuminated by a bank of doublehung windows separated only by wooden uprights. The rooms are connected by large folding doors that tend to increase the effect of brightness. The house is built of brick and decorated with tiles, each of which bears the same design: a large sunflower in high relief. The small corner balconies resemble metal baskets and show an Arabian influence. The Romantic tower, which rises above a portico supported by heavy columns, is decorated with floral and zoomorphic forms. The upper part of the tower houses a small observatory.

10 ''El Capricho''

Palacio Güell, Barcelona
(Figs. 11–20)

Gaudí built this town palace for his patron and later close friend Count Eusebio Güell in 1885–1890. The location is rather unusual for a manorial estate: Conde del Ansalto, located near the major commercial street of La Rambla, does not offer the splendid surroundings desirable for a palatial structure. But despite the seemingly unsuitable site and the relatively small lot (18 × 22 meters) [59 × 72 feet], Gaudí managed to achieve the palatial character required. This manor house served not only as living quarters but also as private museum for the Güell family's large and valuable art collection. In a short time it became a focal point in Barcelona's social life and was renowned for its cultural events such as musical soirées and poetry readings. Gaudí prepared twenty-five drafts for the façade design, but submitted only two to his client. Güell chose the one that Gaudí himself preferred, and this design was then carried out without any major changes. In its structure, the façade is reminiscent of Venetian town palaces. Gaudí had no particular preference for this type of building, but he did want to create the greatest possible harmony between the building (Fig. 11) and its inhabitants. Eusebio Güell's mother was Italian, a Baclgalupi from Genoa; and the palace's Italian elements can be seen as a tribute to the national origin of the house's occupants.

The palace has six stories. There are a few load-bearing walls in the basement, but the building is supported primarily by columns. This arrangement provides excellent ventilation which is further improved by a patio and by ventilating shafts that lead all the way from the basement to the roof (Fig. 12). In addition to housing the stables, the basement contained a tack room and rooms for the grooms. A ramp provided access for the animals, and a spiral staircase provided access for the personnel (Fig. 13). The servants' quarters were at street level. A double gate facilitated the entry of carriages, and narrow stone platforms made it easy to mount the horses (Fig. 14). The kitchen had a garbage chute that ran into the basement. A boldly sweeping iron

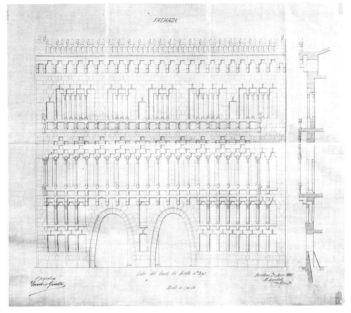

11   Palacio Güell. Elevation of the façade

staircase led to the servants' entrance. The main entrance was by way of an open staircase that led directly to the administrative rooms, the library, and the reception room; an extension of this stairway led to the main floor. The drawing room, which was located in the center of the *piano nobile* [main floor of a Renaissance palace], was roofed with a parabolic vault topped by a conical cupola (Fig. 15). This room, which replaced the traditional patio, played the most important role in the life of the occupants for two reasons: first, because the palace's unfavorable site obliged the occupants to focus their activities toward the center of the building and, secondly, because the drawing room was where the family gave its many parties and concerts and where it held its religious services as well. An altar was concealed behind closet-like doors, and when these doors were opened the drawing room was converted into an oratory with a small sacristy. The location of the organ pipes in the upper galleries surrounding the room gave the organ a magnificent tone.

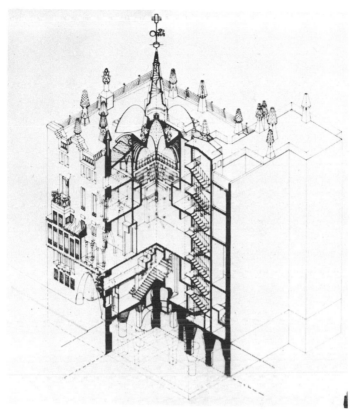

12   Palacio Güell. Axial projection

The front hall that ran parallel to the rear of the building provided access to the rooms located around the drawing room (Fig. 16). A sitting room in the rear of the building received indirect light from windows placed between the load-bearing walls and from openings in the cupola. The remaining stories contained several bedrooms, and there were additional rooms for servants on the top floor. In the center of the roof terrace, which can be used for strolling and lounging, is the 15-meter spire that crowns the drawing room cupola. The spire is surrounded by glazed skylights that provide interior lighting. The eigh-

13   Palacio Güell. Basement

teen imaginatively designed ventilation chimneys are distributed around this central structure (Fig. 18). Every room in this carefully designed and expensively furnished house imparts a different sense of space. But despite this, the individual rooms are precisely coordinated in their decor and blend smoothly into each other. The decoration of the ceilings again reveals the Venetian influence; columns and parabolic arches in the interior resemble those along the street façade (Fig. 19). Thus, the key elements in the ornamentation of the façade anticipate the decor of the living quarters.

One of Gaudí's main interests was in the expressiveness and liveliness of wall surfaces. He gave his buildings "skins" whose optical uniqueness derived from the constant interplay of contrasting surfaces. The street side of the Palacio Güell, in which polished gray marble is superimposed on the stone and brick walls, is severe and noble. The main accent is provided by the gallery overhang located in front of the main floor and supported by stone corbels. It is fascinating to note here how Gaudí, making no use of three-dimensional ornamentation, nonetheless achieved the sense of "motion" he wanted solely by means of the two parabolic arches of the entrance gates and the parabolic, colored glass windows (Fig. 17). The lower parts of the gate grills are made of intertwining geometric patterns that prevent passersby from looking in; the upper portions are executed in a free-flowing ornamental pattern resembling a whiplash. Taken as a whole, the gates are masterpieces of wrought-iron work. An ironwork device between the arches bears witness to Gaudí's Catalan allegiance. It represents the Catalan escutcheon, surrounded by lambrequins and crowned by an eagle.

The building's owner, Count Güell, had come into contact with William Morris and his disciples during his business trips to England; and following Morris's lead, he had decorated several walls of his house in Comillas (in northern Spain) with plant designs. Gaudí was a frequent guest at Count Güell's house and became familiar with art theories in the rest of Europe through Güell and his extensive library of foreign publications. The intertwining floral patterns of the ironwork—which harmonizes beautifully with the marble also used in the interior—are reminiscent of later designs of the Belgian Art Nouveau architect Victor Horta.

14   Palacio Güell. Vestibule with entrance steps and steps for mounting horses ▷

16 Palacio Güell. Corridor with view of the dining hall
◁ 15 Palacio Güell. View of the cupola of the central living room

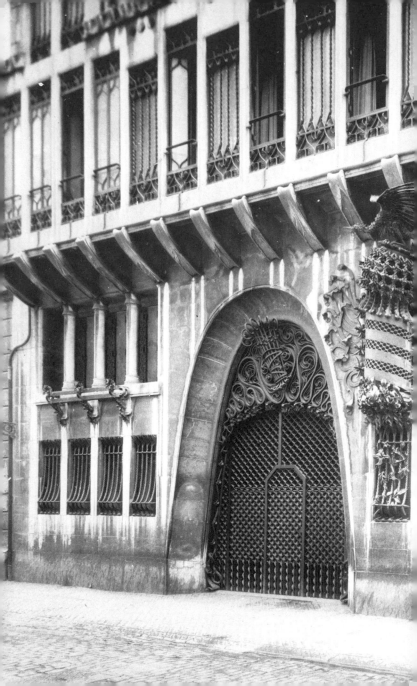

18 Palacio Güell. Overall view of the roof terrace with ventilator, chimneys, and the conical tower that covers the parabolic cupola of the central living room

◁ 17 Palacio Güell. Entrance gates

19 Palacio Güell. Partial view of panel work on the ceiling of the drawing
room facing the main façade

The wealth of ornamental motifs that blend together here to form a harmonious whole testifies to Gaudí's visionary creative powers. In the interior decor of Palacio Güell, Gaudí succeeds in his attempt to combine "incompatible" forms into organic units. One key example of this can be seen in the meshing of arches and capitals (Fig. 20), decorated with plant designs executed in wrought iron. Inlays of various types of wood contrast with gilded wrought iron, tortoise shell with copper work. The painter Alejo Clapés did the colorful, decorative painting in the palace; a large fresco by this artist originally covered the side façade. But the most colorful "painting" in the entire building was done on the chimneys and ventilation shafts on the roof. These structures resemble conically shaped sculptures or decorative elements borrowed from nature. Covered with fragments of colored and patterned tiles, they are early examples of Gaudí's unique approach to form and color (Fig. 18). When the palace was finished, the Catalan press printed some articles on it, most of them with illustrations. None, however, mentioned the architect's name. People were at a loss as to how to react to so much expressiveness. On January 11, 1891, a journalist wrote in *La Illustración Hispano-Americana:* "This architecture differs completely from anything we have ever seen in this city."

◁ 20   Palacio Güell. Interior view of the gallery from the living and dining room

Finca Güell, Barcelona
(Figs. 21–23)

In 1887, Gaudí began to remodel the property that the Güell family owned outside Barcelona between Les Corts de Sarria and Pedralbes. The work was done concurrently with the work on Palacio Güell. The character of the property, which used to be in the country, has now been destroyed by urban sprawl. "Generalissimo Franco" Avenue divides the land of the former Finca Güell. The pavilions and stables are on land now occupied by the City University campus built at the end of the 1920s in the immediate vicinity of the law faculty. The main entrance—the so-called "dragon gate," and one of Gaudí's most popular works—is located on Avenida de la Victoria. Like Gaudí's other buildings, it was built with natural stone and bricks. It has a small side door for pedestrians. Between two posts, one of which is ten meters [32.8 feet] high and serves as a counterweight to the opened gate, are the wrought-iron gate itself and a small wall that screens the pedestrian entrance (Fig. 23). The wall has a textile-like design. Yellow and red bricks are placed in an alternating pattern, and the mortared joints are covered with colored glass chips that reflect the sunlight. The higher post is topped by a flowing crown done in a style akin to Art Nouveau. The lower part of the gate, which is five meters wide, consists of two interlocking geometrical patterns. One is formed by rods running diagonally. The other is made up of squares stamped with a rose pattern. By contrast, the upper half is completely free in its conception. A three-dimensional dragon with double wings guards the entrance (Fig. 21). When the gate is opened, the dragon lifts its claw—which is moved by a chain linkage—as if it wanted to defend the property. In

21   Finca Güell. "Dragon gate" at the main entrance   ▷

22   Finca Güell. Main entrance with "dragon gate," stable, and riding school   ▷

this dragon gate, Gaudí brought the wrought-iron technique, that had been at home in Catalonia since the Middle Ages, to artistic perfection. He combined rolled, cast, and wrought iron and used a wire net for the dragon's wings.

The dragon was one of Gaudí's favorite motifs, and he used it again and again as a decorative element. We find Gaudí alluding to it symbolically in the gigantic reptilian back on the roof of Casa Batlló (Fig. 59); and he used it in Christian form, so to speak, in the devil's dragon that places a bomb in the hand of an anarchist worker and is part of a group of figures in that same house.

The top of the enclosure wall at Finca Güell is lavishly decorated; small arches, incorporating stone corbel bands, open cornices, and a triangular tracery pattern, form a hexagonal ornament that is decorated in turn with colored ceramic pieces displaying the most varied motifs.

The pavilion to the left of the main gate consists of three parts: to either side of an octagonal, single-story building with a cupola roof stand two rectangular towers also topped by cupolas.

The "skin" of what used to be a gatekeeper's house, although conceived linearly, has no flat surfaces. Modeled brick and terra cotta, forming the most varied patterns, achieve a vivid *chiaroscuro* effect almost three-dimensional in character. The roof is built according to the same principle. The ventilation units, cupolas, and lantern reveal Gaudí's genius for form and color, a genius that would celebrate a dramatic and spectacular triumph in the roof superstructure of the Casa Milá (Figs. 71, 73, 74, 76).

On the right side of the gate is a pavilion that was used as a stable (Fig. 22). Its square hall is roofed with wide, parabola-shaped arches, while the neighboring rotunda, with the lantern, accommodated a riding academy. The façade, inspired by the Mudéjar style, is made of air-dried brick mixed with baked bricks and reinforced by visible pillars and lateral bands. To protect the structure against moisture, it was placed on a foundation of quarry stone and is covered with ornamented semicircular stone plates. The ancient Mediterranean tradition of adobe houses inspired Gaudí to fill the hollow spaces between the corner bricks, along the cornices, and so on, with clay. Rainwater, carried by roof channels designed to collect it, runs off over the corners into a

◁ 23 Finca Güell. Entrance and "dragon gate"

fountain. The window frames are formed by brick arches that are stepped at the top.

On the roofs of the Güell pavilion we find cylindrical arches alternating with elliptical and parabolic ones and stair-like structures blending into horizontal and bow-shaped elements. The ceramic mosaic facing on the walls, dominated by blues, whites, and greens, gleams with color.

Among the improvements that Gaudí added to the old manor house (which is now the Pedralbes palace) were an outdoor stairway and a tower-like chimney, both of which displayed the same richness of form we find in the pavilions. Some of these improvements were removed when King Alfonso XIII took over the building.

Episcopal Palace, Astorga
(Figs. 24, 25)

In 1887, Juan Grau, Bishop of Astorga, who came from Gaudí's hometown of Reus, commissioned Gaudí to rebuild the old episcopal residence, which had been destroyed by fire. Catalan builders were brought to the old and venerable city in the northern part of Spain so that they "would be able to execute Gaudí's ideas down to the last detail." The building shows more clearly than any other the influence of the Gothic style on Gaudí's work, as well as his precise knowledge of the writings of Viollet-le-Duc. As Gaudí saw this project, however, the factors demanding a medieval conception were more intellectual than architectural. He chose to build a feudalistic residence that would dominate over the province as its spiritual and religious center and, at the same time, that would stand in contrast to the city's Renaissance architecture. Once again, symbolism, structure, and utility are combined in this building to form a complete synthesis.

Work on the palace went forward, subject to two markedly different influences. On the one hand, the deep bond that Gaudí felt with his client, Juan Grau, who was an unusual and open-minded man, made this project a fruitful and positive experience for the architect. But on the other hand, Gaudí was plagued by disputes with the conservative department of architecture in Madrid. This department showed little understanding for his ideas and, from the very beginning, led him to fear, with good reason, that he would not be able to complete the building.

The palace consists of a rectangular core with a cylindrical tower at each corner. The entrance portico with the throne room above it and the oratory with its three apses protrude (Fig. 24). The basement is surrounded by a moat that provides lighting and ventilation. Above it rise the ground, main, and top floors. Despite the small area that it takes in, the building creates an impression of monumentality, and its unity derives from the upward sweep of its Gothic verticality (Fig. 25). Gaudí rejected the bishop's proposal to use an ostentatious polished

24   Episcopal Palace, Astorga. Entrance portico

25 Episcopal Palace, Astorga. Apse

stone, and he made the inside walls and the vaults, columns, and pillars of brick, which he then varnished. The bases of the polychromatic columns rest on natural stone. For the outside walls, Gaudí selected white granite from the Bierzo Mountains in order to set the palace off against the dark background of the cathedral and the city wall. The white marble had religious connotations, too, symbolizing the white of the bishop's robes and creating a brilliant focal point in the landscape. Still, Gaudí's choice of white drew vehement criticism. No one seemed to realize that the pyramidal roof Gaudí was planning would have created, when covered by winter snows, a color harmony of incomparable beauty.

After the sudden death of Bishop Grau in 1893, Gaudí gave up the project shortly before the roof was to be put on. Not until 1907 did Bishop Julian Diego y Alcolea commission the Madrid architect Luis de Guereta to complete the building. De Guereta ignored Gaudí's plans and so made a harmonious structure impossible. These unfortunate circumstances prevented the residence from actually being used until 1961.

Colegio Teresiano, Barcelona
(Figs. 26, 27)

In 1888–1890, at the same time that he was working on the luxurious Palacio Güell, Gaudí built the home of the Order of St. Theresa of Avila on Calle de Gauduxer in Barcelona. Through his close friend Francisco Marsal, Gaudí had received the commission from Reverend Ossó, with whom he maintained constant contact during the period of construction. This relationship was not always an easy one, since Gaudí had to observe the order's rule of frugality, and this was often at odds with his desire for artistic perfection. One day, when Ossó raised serious objections to the mounting bills, Gaudí replied, unmoved: "To each his own, Reverend Enrique. I build houses, you celebrate the mass and preach." His concept of religion and religious buildings drew on sources other than liturgical regulations. In 1912, Gaudí rejected another offer from the order to build, with certain simplifications, a church he had already designed.

Nevertheless, Gaudí's attempt to achieve a specifically Christian art is clearly evident in the Colegio Teresiano. The spiritual concepts of the saint of Avila were thoroughly compatible with the structural rationality that Gaudí so much admired in Gothic buildings. This rationality finds its most effective expression in the spare and "noble" design of the façade, which is built of unplastered natural stone accented with horizontal brick bands. The high, narrow windows—framed on the upper floor in parabolic arches—give the structure its pronounced Gothic quality (Fig. 26). For a welcoming gesture toward the approaching visitor, as it were, Gaudí placed a small structural component on the front of the building. On the ground floor, this component serves as a lobby and, on the upper floors, as an observation deck. The exterior of the building and its rectangular ground plan with its long, parallel hallways create an effect of restrained and noble simplicity; and the

26   Colegio Teresiano. Rear view ▷

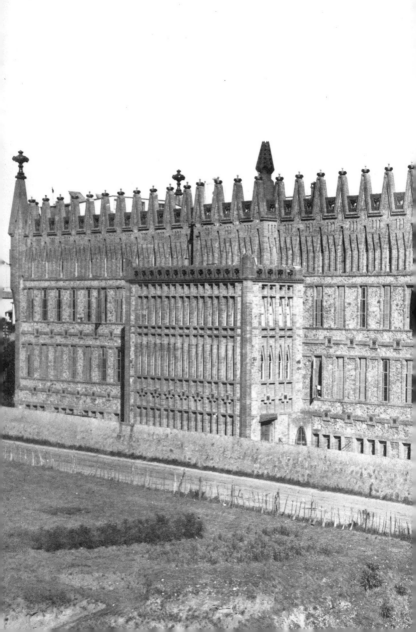

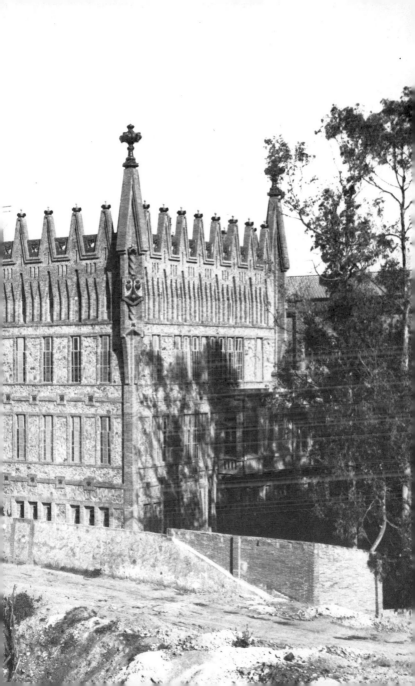

interior intensifies this impression of spare, spiritualized form. The long corridors with their deep perspectives present a seemingly endless chain of parabolically curved arches, and they provide an ideal setting for the nuns who walk along them, sunk in meditation. The vaults, like the rest of the inside walls, are made of brick and display Gaudí's mastery in handling this traditional Catalan construction material. Furthermore, a system of brick arches was the cheapest structural method Gaudí could use and was therefore in keeping with the order's principles. There is no doubt that Gaudí achieved the desired goal in this building: a maximal mystical aura at minimal construction cost.

In his decorative work, Gaudí refrained from using the brilliant colors and oriental ornamentation he had used in his other early buildings. Here he restricted himself to symbolic decorations: The name of Jesus appears 127 times in ceramics, 35 times in wrought iron; the initials of St. Theresa appear 96 times in ceramics and six times in wrought iron. We find the doctoral hat of the order's founder 91 times and her coat of arms six times.

The wrought-iron grille of the parabolic entrance gate is one of the major achievements of Gaudí's early career. The three-part gate is crowned in the middle by an elegant cross that gathers together the lively contours of the twisted iron bands (Fig. 27).

◁ 27   Colegio Teresiano. Wrought-iron gate of the main entrance

57

Casa Calvet, Barcelona
(Figs. 28–32)

In 1897, the sons of the textile manufacturer Pedro Martin Calvet commissioned Gaudí to build a townhouse at 48 Calle de Caspe. In his plans Gaudí followed the same basic scheme he had used in 1891 in Lèon for the Casa de los Botines on the Plaza San Marcolo. The lower floors were taken up by office space; the second floor or "belle étage" contained the owner's apartment; and the rental apartments were located in the upper stories. The houses Gaudí had built in Léon, however, were freestanding. In Barcelona, he had the problem of integrating the façade into an already existing row of houses.

Construction began in March 1898 and was completed in the following year. In June 1900, Gaudí was awarded the prize of the City of Barcelona for this remarkable new structure. In the citation for the award, the judges stressed not only the originality and beauty of the architecture but also the modern solutions Gaudí had found in the areas of sanitation and ventilation.

It has been assumed until recently that Casa Calvet was completed in 1904, but that cannot be the case if Gaudí received a prize for it in 1900. Nor is it likely that the structural work was done by 1900 and that it took another four years to complete the finish work.

Gaudí's buildings up to this point had displayed Gothic and Arabic influences; but in the façade of Casa Calvet he developed a completely new and personal style. Functionality and Baroque exuberance come together here to produce both schematic clarity and lively ornamentation (Fig. 28).

The outside walls are made of cut stone, the inside ones of brick. The structural unity of Casa Calvet is achieved by means of iron girders laid across the supporting beams of the basement, and the walls of the four-story central courtyard rest on the foundation pillars in the base-

◁ 28 Casa Calvet. Façade

30   Casa Calvet. Mirror and tiling in the vestibule

ment (Fig. 29). The arrangement of the rooms is relatively conservative; but in matters of detail, Gaudí created a highly personal style in
Casa Calvet. The columns, for example, were made to look like trees.
This is one of Gaudí's first attempts to incorporate motifs inspired by
nature into architectural reality. The brasswork was thoroughly in keeping with the linear style of Art Nouveau (Fig. 30).

The main features of the quasi–rusticated façade are the small balconies that rest on Baroque consoles and the bay window located over
the main entrance and decorated with the family coat of arms and a
cypress, the symbol of hospitality (Fig. 31). The two gables act as

◁ 29   Casa Calvet. Patio with elevator and staircase

31   Casa Calvet. Oriel in the façade

focal points for the building, which caused Gaudí some worry because the authorities had warned him that the building could not exceed an "appropriate" height. Thanks to the political influence of his client, who was, like Gaudí himself, a convinced Catalan, Gaudí was able to execute his original plan. The gables are topped by two crosses, which are difficult to make out from the street. They prompted Countess Güell to ask the architect just what those "complicated looking things" were. Gaudí's reply is typical for his style of humor. "Two crosses," he said, "and they have caused a lot of people no end of complications and annoyance."

32   Casa Calvet. Rear view ▷

There was also trouble with the nuns of an adjoining convent who pushed through an injunction to prevent their view from being blocked. Gaudí found an architectonic solution to this problem, building the wall of the interior courtyard in a sequence of arches placed at a slight angle. They permit daylight to come in and at the same time screen the convent.

The simple rear façade is altogether modern in its conception: The balconies are alternately concave and convex, alternately open and glassed in (Fig. 32). Despite the functional simplicity of the building, a simplicity that is evident too in the practical arrangement of the apartments, Gaudí also indulges his predilection for symbolic detail. The family saints, in decorative settings, appear just as frequently as the inscription "Patria, Fe, Amor" [Fatherland, Faith, Love]. Particularly noteworthy in this respect is a wrought-iron door knocker. Shaped like a cross, the symbol of the divine, the knocker beats upon the back of a louse, the symbol of depravity, whenever anyone seeks entry.

Bellesguard, Barcelona
(Figs. 33–35)

Doña Maria Sagues, the widow of Figuera, one of Gaudí's greatest admirers, commissioned him in 1900 to build her a mansion in the country. The piece of land near Barcelona she chose was known as "Bellesguard," i.e., "beautiful view." (Today this lot is 16 Calle de Bellesguard.) Barcelona's last king, Martin I, had a summer home built here in 1408. Located in the foothills of Mt. Tibado, the spot is certainly deserving of its name. From it, one looks across hills and gardens toward Barcelona and can watch the ships heading into port. Catalonia is revealed here in all of its beauty, and it is only natural that Gaudí, in view of this location and its historical background, selected a building style reminiscent of the glorious age of his beloved homeland.

The crenellated house (Fig. 33) with its Gothic windows and pointed spire topped by a four-armed cross (Fig. 34) is in the medieval palace tradition. The archetype of color harmony Gaudí worked toward—a merging of structure and environment, the organically rooted building as art form—is attained in the perfect adaptation of "Bellesguard" to the landscape. The interplay of colors, ranging from dark brown to ocher, in the stonework and the multicolored patio window (Fig. 35) blend harmoniously with the shrubbery and pines of the grass-covered slope. In contrast to the angular appearance of the exterior, the interior is all smooth-flowing lines. All the ceilings make use of the same theme but vary it with great ingenuity, their arches and vaults producing compositions in light and shadow. The top floor is a masterpiece, Resembling a truncated pyramid from the outside, it constitutes the most interesting part of the building. Instead of load-bearing inside walls, there are brick pillars that become wider at the top and form masonry platforms. From these protrude triple corbel arches that then widen in the gallery into a series of ceiling arches. In the side galleries the arches are flatter and rest perpendicularly on the vaults of the lower façade walls. The elements of these arches do not form a solid mass

34   Villa "Bellesguard." Façade

but are interspersed with a triangular tracery pattern that makes the structure appear light. Above them is a flat masonry ceiling forming the base of the pyramid, which contains a storeroom with "Tabicada vaulting."

Whenever possible, Gaudí designed his arches in such a way that the thrust would be supported by load-bearing walls. In the upper stories of Bellesguard, where the walls are thin, he used machined iron bracing that took up the thrust and was not hidden under masonry but was deliberately left exposed.

This complex architecture can be appropriately described by the paradoxical term "simple complexity." What may strike the observer

◁ 33   Villa "Bellesguard." Rear view

35 Villa "Bellesguard." Patio window

as a cleverly devised system of braces and loads was, for the architectural genius Gaudí, merely the perception and realization of formal harmony. The comparatively conservative arrangement of floors and rooms is enlivened by the octagonal entrance patio that rises to a height of three stories.

Bellesguard represents an intermediate stage in Gaudí's artistic development. The ceilings, the freely plaited wrought iron in the main gate, and the color harmony signal his break with traditional architectural principles.

Chapel at Santa Coloma
(Figs. 36–39)

In 1898, Don Eusebio Güell commissioned one of Gaudí's colleagues, Francisco Berenguer, to build a textile factory with an adjoining housing development for workers in Santa Coloma de Cervelló south of Barcelona. The count set great store by this project, and the master himself was assigned the task of designing the chapel for the settlement. Gaudí was devoting more and more of his attention to the problem of chapel construction as an expression of religious feeling, and he spent ten years in making sketches, models, and calculations before work on the chapel actually began in 1908. The building site was at the foot of a low hill surrounded by woods; in making his

36 Chapel, Santa Coloma de Cervelló. Interior view of the crypt

37 Chapel, Santa Coloma de Cervelló. Rough sketch, showing Gaudí's conception of the completed chapel

calculations, Gaudí considered not only the access road to the chapel but also its integration into the surroundings and landscape. However, the form of this structure, which is probably Gaudí's finest work, is the product not only of mathematical computations but also of Gaudí's remarkable spatial sensitivity. Routine drafting procedures proved inadequate to this task and gave way to the preparation of models. Gaudí developed a method very much his own for solving the design problems. He constructed an upside-down model, made of cords and small weights with the latter representing the loads to be supported and the cords representing the arches and pillars of the new building. The architect arrived at the forms he wanted by suspending weights—bags filled with lead shot—from wires; these weights were proportional to the estimated loads and thrusts. The weight of the little bags could easily be adjusted by adding or removing shot. This model was suspended from boards or from the ceiling. When the entire arrangement was turned upside-down, the location of the suspended loads indicated the shape of the vault and the vertical location of the supports. The points where the wires were attached in the model corresponded to the bases of the pillars in the planned structure. This procedure made it

38   Chapel, Santa Coloma de Cervelló. Crypt entrance, steps, and porch

39   Chapel, Santa Coloma de Cervelló. Exterior view of the crypt

possible for Gaudí to determine the inverted mechanical structure. The suspended model was photographed and then painted a reddish, brick-like color to aid in visualizing the spatial effect, and the resulting parabolic curves were computed later by graphic methods.

A drawing by Gaudí—the final phase in the experiments described above—shows the design for the completed chapel (Fig. 37). Although all the details are not worked out in this drawing, the formal concept is clear—the desire to blend together all the individual elements, such as the columns, vaults, and walls. The result, strictly speaking, can no longer be considered Gothic or influenced solely by the Gothic style; indeed, by dispensing with the buttress system and by using the hyperbolic paraboloid as the basic form and curved surfaces throughout the entire building in the walls, ceilings, and columns, Gaudí departed from all traditional styles.

The function of the Gothic flying buttresses, which Gaudí always scorned as a "crutch," is taken over by diagonal supports. No two pillars are identical; they are inclined in various directions and ramified in various ways, and they differ from each other in form and material. The columns do not follow any regular pattern either; their cross sections vary in accordance with the shapes of the ceiling vaults and the resultant loads. The walls are curved and inclined, too; and it is the curvature of these hyperbolic paraboloids that gives the building its required structural rigidity. For the actual construction of the crypt, the nave, and the vestibule Gaudí used a traditional Catalan method of construction—vaults with brick walls. At structural junctions, the supporting elements are built of dark bricks baked hard and of narrow, horizontally placed stones. This combination yields a vaguely triangular pattern. Inserted into the corners are glazed tiles that lend a decorative accent without obscuring the structure. The ribs of the vaults consist of bricks placed on edge for maximum load-bearing efficiency with minimal volume. The columns near the entrance are fully plastered; others are only partially plastered; and the remaining ones are made of brick laid in varying patterns (Fig. 36). In the center of the nave are four basalt columns, each made of a single piece of stone, that are striking in their expressiveness. It is obvious that Gaudí wanted his building materials to be visible and that variations in the "stone fabric" of the building were his only decorative elements.

The construction of the extremely complicated chapel required so much craftsmanship that the building process deserves to be considered a work of art in its own right. Texture and form, however, do not imitate nature; it is nature that dictates texture and form. This is particularly clear in the vestibule. The effect created by daylight entering between the tree-like pillars and being reflected back by the vaults in the interior of the chapel conveys a sense of life to the architecture and seems to link the form of the pillars with that of the pines in the surrounding woods, suggesting that both pillars and trees have a common formal ancestry (Fig. 38). The simple patterns in the stained glass windows were also inspired by natural forms, and their leafy contours are in keeping with the unusual technique of their construction. Fine grillwork protects the glass without impairing its visual effect. In this grillwork, Gaudí made use of some unorthodox materials, such as discarded parts from machines for spinning cotton (Fig. 39). This feature again demonstrates the indissoluble unity of architecture, life, and human productivity in Gaudí's works.

Park Güell, Barcelona
(Figs. 40–52)

Park Güell is a work of art unique in its diversity. This successful synthesis of architecture, sculpture, and color, of nature, space, and light attests to the visionary power of a brilliant architect. Also evident in it are Gaudí's skill in city planning and his grasp of what makes a suitable environment for man. In these respects he was far ahead of his time and can serve as a model for us today.

Planning and Design

In 1900, Eusebio Güell i Bacigalupi, Gaudí's patron, supporter, and friend, commissioned him to design a "garden suburb" with a residential character. The Count admired the English housing developments of this kind and hoped, in vain as it turned out, to win the support of Barcelona's residents for this project. The site was on a bare hill 150 meters [492 feet] above sea level—the Montaña Pelada, or "treeless mountain"—in the northwest of the city. Gaudí carefully studied the topography of this rather unpromising "material" and attached great importance during the entire project to preserving the natural contours of the mountain. The park takes in 15 hectares [37 acres] and was to be divided into some 60 individual lots all of which were to be located in the areas receiving maximum sunlight. The triangular parcels were arranged in a square in such a way that the houses to be built in the center of each triangle would not block each other's view of Barcelona lying at the foot of the hill. The remaining area was to be used for a park and community facilities.

This splendid project proved, however, to be a financial disaster. Only two parcels were sold, and only two houses were built: one by the lawyer Don Martin Trias Domenech and the other, in 1906, by Gaudí himself. Gaudí occupied the house, designed by his technical expert Francisco Berenguer, with his elderly father and his niece. The

75

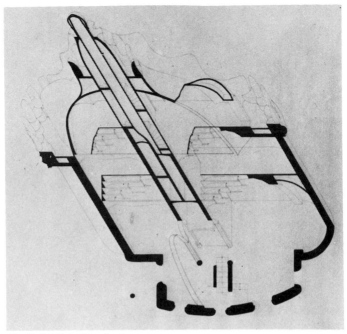

40 Park Güell. Plan for the entranceway

41 Park Güell. Administrative pavilion, to the left of the main entrance ▷
76

42   Park Güell. Gatekeeper's house

park thus remained a private garden until the 1920's, when the Güell family turned it over to the city for a public recreation area.

The Situation Today

The center of the park is enclosed by a wall that follows the natural shape of the hill and has seven gates. It was supposed to give the residents a sense of protection and security since at the beginning of the century the park was rather isolated. The section of the wall that is of greatest artistic interest lies on Calle de Olot, near the main entrance. The lower part is of natural stone; vertical corbel bands of rusticated stone support the double curvature of the coping, which is covered with a smooth mosaic to prevent anyone from climbing over it. The decorative overlay of glass and ceramic fragments presents the eye with an inexhaustible variety of color and form. Basically unimposing patterns are combined to create an overall picture of great vitality. The mosaic inscription "Park Güell" appears repeatedly in medallions set into the wall. The undecorated sections of the wall incorporate pillars that are topped by flower pots and that reflect the shape of the palms on the other side of the street. Gaudí's integration of his work into the natural surroundings is elevated to an architectonic principle here. The main entrance is located between two pavilions. The grating of the gate is made of angle iron to which a palm-leaf design in cast-iron is bolted (Fig. 40).

Both entrance pavilions are of brown rubble and have an oval ground plan. One serves as a gatehouse, the other as an administration building (Figs. 41, 42). The window openings are bordered with reddish-white and bluish-white mosaics, and the convex glass of the over-sized windows of the administrative pavilion are covered with iron meshwork. In the centers of the domed roofs, which are finished with vitrified tiles, are large ventilation shafts surrounded by merloned lookout platforms (Fig. 43). The modeling of the roofs and of certain detail structures is accented by color. One pavilion is adorned with a 10 meter [32.8 foot] high tower whose bluish-white patterns harmonize perfectly with the colors of the sky (Figs. 41, 44). The tower ends in the familiar cross with four branches and is a classic example of Gaudí's intuitive sense for the equilibrium of shapes. In form, the tower is a helicoid—the geometrical pattern on which screw threads are based—and the rectangles superimposed on it lend rhythm to it.

On entering the park, one stands before a sweeping stairway and its bordering walls decorated with lavishly colorful merlons (Fig. 45). The shimmering surfaces of the glazed tile fragments contrast with the natural stone and are cast into especially bold relief by the dark background of the bushes and trees. Squares and rectangles, alternately concave and convex, lend a three-dimensional accent to the lively curve of the side walls. Prefabricated components were used in the stairway as well as in the colonnades and pavilions. The farsighted and inventive architect used reinforced concrete here. This was the first time this material was ever used in Spain.

Two symmetrical stairways, which are separated by plantings, fountains, and zoomorphic sculptures (Fig. 46), lead directly to a large plaza whose lower part was to serve as a market. The upper part was to be a gathering place and forum for cultural events. Underneath the market, a cistern with a capacity of 12,000 liters [3,170 gallons] was installed to collect rainwater. The so-called "Greek Theater," the upper part of the "Plaza," is closed off on its sloping side by a stone bench. Half of the 86 × 40 meter [282 × 131 foot] plaza is on solid ground; the other half rests on colonnades (Fig. 47) that represent Gaudí's tribute to the classical period and his highly personal interpre-

43 Park Güell. Ventilation chimney with merlons on the roof of the gate-keeper's house

44   Park Güell. Roof structure and spire on the administrative pavilion

tation of the Doric order (Fig. 48). The fluted, red sandstone columns—
6 meters [20 feet] high and 1.5 meters [5 feet] in diameter—stand in
harmonious relation to the 2 meter [6.5 foot] high entablature. Between
the columns, reinforced concrete beams subdivide the ceiling into a
square network into which are set domes that cover the remaining space
(Fig. 48). The ceiling is finished in white glass mosaics combined with
pictures at the intersections which are executed in colored glazed tile.

   The outer columns, which lean inward and are tapered, and the
curved entablature are crowned by a cornice of glazed tile which also
forms the bench-like railing of the terrace. The runoff flows from the
cornice—which is also a rain trough—into the interior of the slanted

45   Park Güell. Main entrance and stairway

columns and then on down into the cistern. The curves in the bench
are determined by the locations of the capitals on the columns beneath
it (Fig. 49).

   This serpentine bench can be cited as evidence against those critics
who have unjustly described Gaudí's work as eccentric, abstract, or
misanthropic. Today we would be more likely to say that improving
the quality of life was his primary goal. To obtain the best possible
contour for this bench, Gaudí had a naked worker sit on a plaster mold
that was still wet. Orienting himself by this casting, Gaudí then designed the contour of the bench. In addition, the curves in the bench
encourage people to sit together in small groups and talk.

   The decorative mosaics at Park Güell, probably Gaudí's most important work of this type, serve both artistic and hygenic ends. Gaudí
and his assistant Jujol—moved by economic as well as artistic considerations—collected rejects from first-rate ceramic workshops and then

82

46   Park Güell. Sculptures and fountains on the stairway

47   Park Güell. Main plaza and colonnade ▷

put them together in compositions that anticipate the best collages. Gaudí created his surrealistic images guided solely by his sense of natural color harmony and using such ordinary materials as pieces of broken glass and tableware (Fig. 50).

To create optimum living conditions on the hill, Gaudí separated vehicular and pedestrian traffic by designing a complicated system of roads and footpaths. He routed foot traffic via stairways and paths; and instead of sloping or leveling the ground, he built numerous sections of roadway as viaducts resting on monolithic tilted columns (Fig. 52). Load-bearing walls and viaducts were tested in models that reflected the exact same static forces that would be at work in the real structures. The paths and walks were perfectly adapted to the shape of the hill, but here too, Gaudí went a step further than had the landscape architects of the Romantic period. Slanted pillars serve both as supports and as buttresses. Their shapes and their angles of inclination conform to the special conditions of the vaults, the walls, and the curvatures of the streets they support (Fig. 51). Gaudí closed off grottos and passageways underneath the viaducts with iron gates of simple, elegant design, gates that create the impression of being silhouettes of organic origin.

◁ 48   Park Güell. Colonnades of the "market"

49   Park Güell. Partial view of the benches of the main plaza   ▷

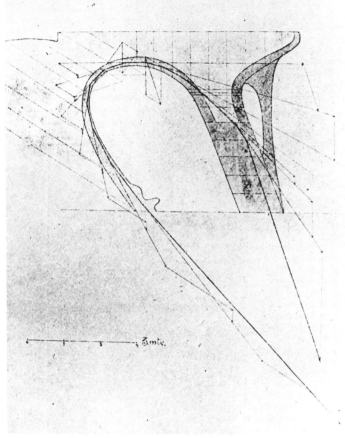

51 Park Güell. Working drawing of the parabolic vault of a viaduct

52 Park Güell. Vault structure of a viaduct ▷

50 Park Güell. View of Barcelona from the main plaza and overlooking the ▷ ▷
benches and gatehouse

Casa Batlló, Barcelona
(Figs. 53–63)

In Casa Batlló, Gaudí's predilection for natural forms is expressed in the modulation of the entire building. The structure determines the whole and its parts; in this house, the "inspired" architecture Gaudí aspired to became reality.

53 Casa Batlló. Ground plan, elevation, and sectional drawing

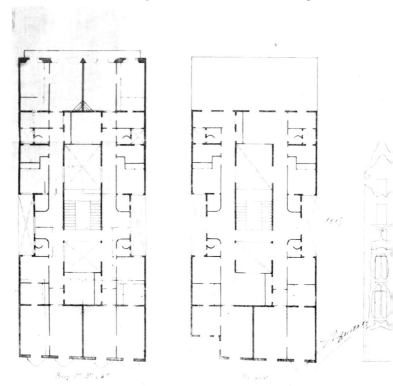

In 1904, the textile manufacturer Batlló commissioned Gaudí to remodel a house in the middle of the Paseo de Gracia, Barcelona's most fashionable street, and gave him a completely free hand. If we look at the official plans, we get the impression that the architect did not want to let the authorities, with whom he had had numerous difficulties before, pin him down to any single solution. Instead, he formulated his ideas in a sketchy way that left various possibilities open if he decided he wanted to make changes in the conception of his three-dimensional façade. Through Gaudí, the monotonous, conservative old

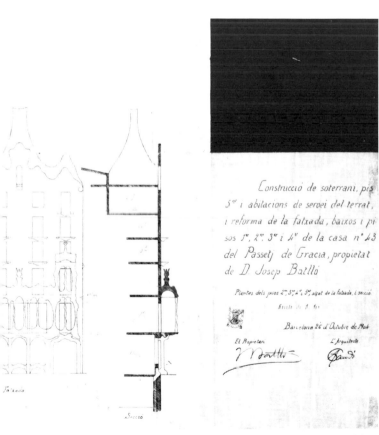

Construcció de soterrani, pis 5^e i abilacions de servei del terrat, i reforma de la fatxada, baixos i pisos 1^e, 2ⁿ, 3^e i 4^t de la casa n° 43 del Passeig de Gracia, propietat de D. Josep Batlló

Plantes dels pisos 2ⁿ, 3^e, 4^t, 5^e, alçat de la fatxada, i secció

Escala de 1: 61

Barcelona 26 d'Octubre de 1906

El Propietari   L'Arquitecte

54 Casa Batlló. Partial
    view of the gallery
    of the façade

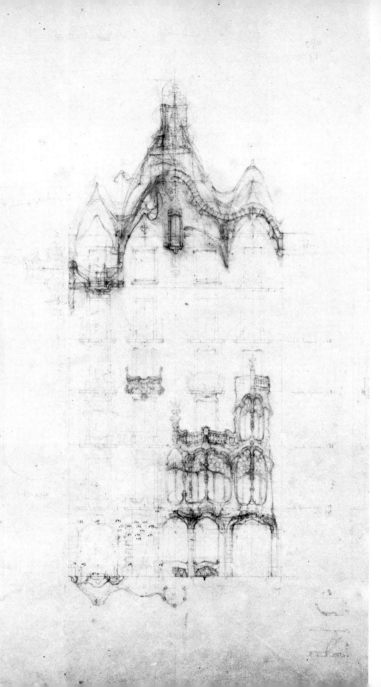

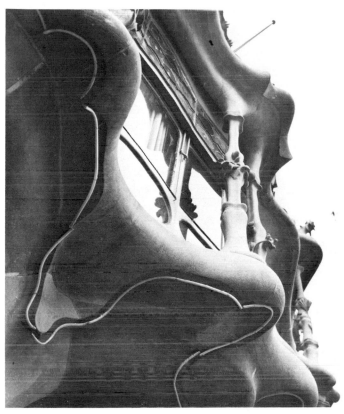

56   Casa Batlló. View from beneath the gallery

59 Casa Batlló. Chimney groups, tower cross, and "reptile's back" on the roof terrace

◁ 58 Casa Batlló. Partial view of the "reptile's back" and tower roof with cross

(Figure 57 on page 103)

house received, in the truest sense of the word, a new face of tremendous vitality and intensity (Fig. 53). To relieve the monotony of the existing façade of four stories with their four rectangular balconies each, Gaudí built five stone arcades at the street level. Above these rises a continuous gallery that extends upward to the next story at its ends and culminates in striking balconies (Fig. 54). Gaudí added the attic and the roof terrace, thus realizing his concept of "crowning" a building. Just as important personages use both a hat and a parasol at the same time, houses, too, should have a double roof. The individual elements of the façade merge across the entire front of the building into a dynamic natural form (Fig. 55) that is also reflected in the harmony of the colors. The superimposed parts are of bright Montjuich stone; and above them, looking like a dinosaur's back, rises the roof of green ceramic tile. The expressive forms of the wrought-iron balconies and the disk-shaped glass mosaics lend a lively accent to the smooth, tile-covered part of the façade. The whole front undulates to emphasize the plasticity of the building and to prevent undesirable reflections (Fig. 56). True to his convictions, Gaudí chose structures found in nature—"the work of the great Master Builder"—as his model for the gallery, which is the major feature of the façade. The gallery has a central window and two side windows, all of which are curved and are supported by bone-like posts that organize and subdivide the composition (Fig. 57). The articulations are concealed by plant-like forms (Fig. 60). The flowing rhythm seems to defy the conventional architectural principles of support and load.

The three-dimensional character of the house is evident in countless details, but above all in the conception of the roof terrace and, indeed, of the whole roof, in which an opening was cut to provide a good view of the Paseo. A small side terrace was added as a lookout. At the end of it and visible from a considerable distance stands a small tower topped by a cross with four branches (Fig. 58). The individual parts of the roof relate to the whole just as the details of a sculpture relate to the whole sculpture. Sweeping lines emerge from the transition of one form into another. What appeared as isolated parts in earlier works

57   Casa Batlló. Façade   ▷

61   Casa Batlló. Interior view of the gallery from the dining room
      (Figure 60 on page 107)

(e.g., the transitions from the columns to the arches of the loggias in Palacio Güell) are fused into a unity here. The plastic forms of the roof railing correspond to those of the chimney clusters, whose surfaces are decorated with colorful mosaics of glazed tile. In terms of color as well as form they were treated as a cluster and not as individual elements (Fig. 59). In his mosaic work, Gaudí adopted the inexpensive, simple method, traditional in Catalan architecture, of using broken pieces of tile left over from the kilns. These tile fragments were well suited to Gaudí's curved surfaces because, in contrast to unbroken tiles intended for flat surfaces, they were much more versatile in their application. Indeed, Gaudí can be considered the inventor of a new style of mosaic work comparable to the "collages" developed by the cubists much later.

Gaudí was also fond of tile as a decorative element for practical reasons. The rugged surface of tile stood up well to the extremes of Barcelona's weather. With tiles that he often broke himself, as well as with shards from old bottles, porcelain, and dolls' heads, he formed surrealistic images consisting only of color and without any clearly recognizable features. Thus, the roof of the Casa Batlló is covered with a colored "skin" almost impressionistic in nature.

Gaudí's plastic view of architecture aided him in remodeling the exterior of the house, around which he could hang, as it were, a new cloak. Although he faced major construction problems in remodeling the interior and the roof, he remained true to his concepts. He placed the roof on an elastic structure of open brick arches that was, in a sense, independent of the rest of the house and did not affect the lower part of the building when it contracted and expanded in response to temperature changes. The arches he added on the ground floor and the gallery above them called for some kind of balancing structure in the upper stories. To avoid overloading the sound wooden pillars in the house, Gaudí went back on his earlier principles and used an "artificial" building material. With reinforced concrete, which had just come into use and which Gaudí jokingly called "iron wood," he was able to give the main stairway the curvature he wanted and to connect the

60   Casa Batlló. Façade window   ▷

62   Casa Batlló. Dining room

ventilating ducts to the façade. He also used steel bolts anchored in the wooden pillars and steel girders to compensate for the increased thrust. The steel elements of the structure remained exposed and were not, as in Gaudí's earlier works, concealed by ornamentation. In the interior, Gaudí's major effort went into renovating the main floor, which his client's family would use as living quarters. Alterations on the other floors were minor.

A spacious vestibule on the street level serves as the entrance to the rental apartments and provides access to the sweeping oak staircase that leads to the main floor (Fig. 63). At the head of the stairs is the reception room. Next comes the living room, which extends along the major part of the gallery; the bedrooms lie to either side of it. One bedroom is separated from the parlor by a wall of glass and wood that features a three-dimensional pattern and harmonizes with the similarly constructed ceiling, which is decorated with a spiral pattern of grooves and bands. Probably the most remarkable room in the living area was the dining room, which has unfortunately been remodeled by the present owner (Fig. 62). From this room with its masterful woodwork and turned pillars a door led to the spacious rear terrace, which afforded a view of the colorful, sweeping galleries and loosely woven ironwork balconies on the rear façade.

The metal and glass doors and the illumination of the stairway by way of two separate patios were highly unusual at the time the house was built. Gaudí extended the windows downward into the stairway patio where the light diminished progressively in the lower stories. Each window had a device in its lower section that provided ventilation even with the window closed. The light shaft itself is decorated with blue ceramic tile in various shades—brighter at the bottom, darker at the top to balance the stronger incidence of light there. The boldly designed windows and glass doors in the lower floors are decorated inside and out with round, irregularly spaced colored glass mosaics. The roof over the interior patio is framed with steel parabolas that support the sloping glass of the skylight. Parabolic arches of masonry work form the rear corridor leading to the terrace. Glass was used not only in the numerous external windows but also in the interior to divide or combine rooms and in skylights, the transparency of which represents an additional architectonic element.

Gaudí's furniture designs for Casa Batlló, drawn in 1907, were revolutionary; they repeat the flowing lines of the building and conform to the shape of the human body. In Casa Batlló, Gaudí achieved his ambitious goal: a blending of functionalism, esthetics, and "nature."

63   Casa Batlló. Vestibule and stairway to the owner's apartment   ▷

Casa Milá, Barcelona
(Figs. 64–76)

Casa Milá—commissioned by the family of the same name—is undoubtedly Gaudí's most important secular building. Free of any historical models, Gaudí's architectural and esthetic concepts reach their apex here. The rectangular lot measured 34 × 56 meters [111.5 × 183.7 feet] and was located at the intersection of Paseo de Gracia and Calle de Provenza. The Calle de Provenza marked the city limits of Gracia before that town was incorported into Barcelona. Gracia now falls within the new residential section of Ensanche. The lot's location called for a kind of double house provided with several entrances and a uniform façade. The blocks in the Ensanche section are laid out diagonally, and the house rows run at an angle of 45 degrees. Gaudí, however, rounded the corners of his building and stressed its free ground plan (Fig. 64). Construction was begun in 1906. Three different plans are still extant, and they are finished down to the last detail as far as the placement of the rooms and the interior design are concerned. The plan of the façade, however, left a number of possibilities open; and Gaudí was no doubt deliberately vague so that he could preclude any interference from the city authorities (Fig. 65). In the rental apartments, Gaudí dispensed with load-bearing walls and built a system of pillars and columns that enabled him to shape each story differently. The apartments—four on each floor—all faced the street. The rooms—which are round, oval, or rounded at the corners—are connected by curved hallways which also lead directly to the surrounding balconies. Thus, the rooms do not have to be used as passageways (Fig. 66). In the plans approved by the city, the luxuriant curves of the corridors were toned down somewhat; and, executed under someone else's supervision, they finally ended up as polygons arranged in a fan pattern. The windows, however, remain faithful to the initial plans, and are placed below floor level so as not to block the view toward the Paseo.

The final form of the façade, which is sketched only vaguely in the submitted plans, is an embodiment in stone of Gaudí's theory. Here,

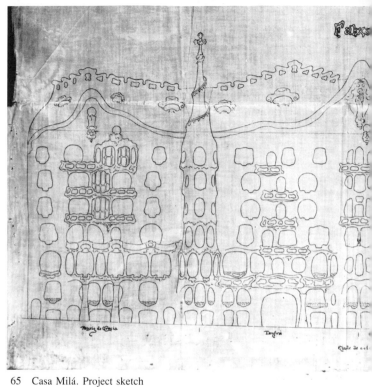

65   Casa Milá. Project sketch

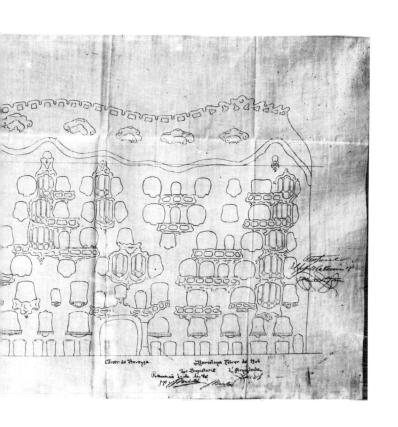

Carrer de Provença.   Barcelona Febrer de 1906

                        Los Propietaris   L'Arquitecte

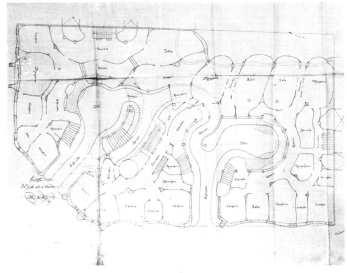

66 Casa Milá. Original ground plan

67 Casa Milá. Façade detail

originality is truly achieved by returning to origins. The front of the building follows serpentine lines that accentuate each story. These "wavy" horizontal bands have their counterparts in the curved horizontals of the capitals and window frames (Fig. 67). The vertical element in the roof was repeated in the ground floor window grills, which have since been removed. This feature increased the three-dimensional quality of the façade. The rounded, cave-like windows, the irregular columns, and the luxuriant plant-like ironwork on the balconies appear to be new inventions of nature (Fig. 68).

Casa Milá has often been called the largest abstract sculpture in the world, and one indeed gets the impression that a single gigantic hand subdued and shaped these masses. The word "construction" is somehow inappropriate here. The enormous façade resembles the sea frozen in motion. The patina of the stone is enhanced by the trailing plants and flowers that grow on the balconies and impart constantly shifting tones of color to the building. As Gaudí himself put it, the cumulative effect of this façade is "the highest expression of a Romantic and anti-Classical artistic will that perceives architecture as a natural event." Collins described Casa Milá as "a man-made mountain." This is a common response, and it has been expressed frequently in various forms. It can be misleading, however, for Gaudí had no intention of "copying" nature. If that had been his intention, he would have carried it out more precisely. Thus the comparison with "surf" that presents itself so readily never gets beyond formalism, for it does not in any way reflect the chaotic aspect of waves rolling and breaking. The very smallest part in Gaudí's work radiates calm and harmony in its relation to the whole. Gaudí's bond with nature found expression not superficially but through his instinct for proportions and for unbroken relationships. "Amis, la nature nous fait: psst, psst!" Le Corbusier wrote in 1948. This remark captures Gaudí's feeling that the secrets of nature reside in its essence and not in its external manifestations.

Regardless of any obvious similarities between Gaudí's work and Art Nouveau, this principle of design makes it clear that Gaudí was not an "Art Nouveau architect." His interest in nature focused on the three-dimensional shape that revealed itself not only in surface motion but also in the forces underlying that motion. He was not primarily interested in the climbing plants and foliage spreading out over a bare wall but rather in the forces animating them. He left the path of naturalism and became an expressionist in the sense that the spiritual element was of primary importance to him. The natural form came second.

The compact, uniform stone surface of the façade of Casa Milá is interrupted only by the glass surfaces of the receding windows, the ironwork of the balconies, and the white ceramic covering of the top floor. The resulting monumentality explains why the building was given the nickname of "La Pedrera" or "stone quarry."

The ramps leading into the basement which connect both parts of the house was a major innovation. Gaudí had used this idea before in Palacio Güell, but here he had room to enlarge on it and provide access for carriages. He was thus the first to create a system that would later be used in multilevel underground garages. The stairways and ramps captured the imagination of the man in the street, and the rumor soon spread that the occupants of Casa Milá could drive their carriages all the way to the front doors of their apartments. Gaudí probably would have chosen that solution today, for he did in fact build an impressive spiral staircase that winds its way up the inside walls of the central courtyard. The stairway in the courtyard, which is bounded only by pillars and windows is dizzying. The stairs appear to be free standing, as if the steps could not find any support. This arrangement stands in direct relationship to the bold superstructures on the roof. A marquee-like iron roof extends over the unbanistered staircase to screen the windows of the adjoining apartments.

The staircase to the patio on the Paseo de Gracia is bordered by a modeled railing accented by jardinières. Plants and flowers blend with the colorful painting of floral decorations that are both raised from and cut into the wall. Two other inside staircases provide quick access to the apartments. The patio on Calle de Provenza also has an unbanistered and roofed stairway that leads into the interior of the second floor.

The concept of living conditions appropriate for human beings was the guiding principle for the entire interior (Fig. 69). The ceilings are particularly noteworthy in this regard. Modeled in free relief or decorated with nearly three-dimensional cement tiles, they give each room its own particular character. There is not one single straight line or flat surface in Casa Milá, and the interplay of light and shadow in the

68   Casa Milá. Entrance portico on the Paseo de Gracia   ▷

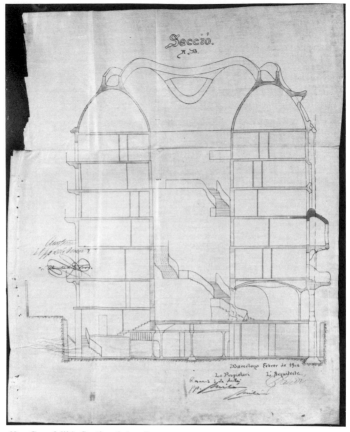

69   Casa Milá. Sectional drawing

vaults at various times of the day gives the building an intense vitality
both inside and out. Numerous details extending over the façade and
on up to the roof superstructures help relate the enclosed space to the
outdoors. The main gate, made of wrought iron fashioned in natural
shapes filled in with small glass panes, connects the building and the
street rather than separating them (Fig. 70). In accordance with the

122

idea of the "third dimension," the balconies extending around the building have built-in benches alternating with planted jardinières.

The entire house rests on free-standing cement or brick columns in conjunction with terra cotta arches and metal framing. There are no supporting walls. The floor of the central patio rests on a star-shaped iron frame which, like many other elements in the house, Gaudí first tested in a scale model. Gaudí waited until the rough-hewn natural stone—in this case, limestone—was in place before he smoothed it, thus blending it into the whole and working more like a sculptor polishing his finished statue. The roof, which is serpentine in form (Fig. 71), is not purely decorative but follows logically from the roof struc-

70   Casa Milá. Entrance gate on the Paseo de Gracia

71 Casa Milá. Roof superstructures and mansard

72 Casa Milá. Attic,
before modification ▷

ture. All the parabolic arches in the roof use the same curve; thus, depending on their span, they will stand higher or lower (Fig. 72). Where the attic is wider, the arches are correspondingly higher; this produces the sweeping line of the roof (Fig. 75). The parabolic arches are built of bricks placed on edge. This provides maximum stability with minimum thickness (15 centimeters) [6 inches]. The attic was later converted into apartments.

The roof superstructures, which combine to form an abstract surrealist scene, are executed with simplicity that anticipates the best sculptural works of the twentieth century (Fig. 73). The chimneys and ventilation shafts over the staircase exits were conceived like parts of a monumental sculpture and frequently remind us of human forms (Figs. 74, 76). They are covered with fragments of white or gray tile or with terra cotta. By this time Gaudí had already developed his preference for subdued colors that do not overburden the expressive forms he derived from curved surfaces. The chimneys and shafts were originally conceived as parts of a large central group that was to feature a statue of the Virgin Mary. But this plan was never carried out. In the anti-religious demonstrations of the "week of tragedy" in July 1909, most of Barcelona's convents and monasteries went up in flames; and the Milá family decided to forego any visible religious symbols in order to avoid difficulties. This disturbed Gaudí deeply, and it is certainly the reason why he did not complete this unusual work. His ablest collaborators—the architects Bayo, Canaleta, and Sugrañes—completed the structure, but were unable to fully implement Gaudí's ideas.

73   Casa Milá. Ventilation chimney and exits to the roof terrace ▷

74   Casa Milá. Ventilation chimneys

76   Casa Milá. Ventilation chimney ▷

La Sagrada Familia, Barcelona
(Figs. 77–95)

The ambitious project of building a large votive church in honor of the Holy Family originated with José Mario Bocabella y Verdaguer, the owner of a religious bookstore and the author of Christian writings. The idea was inspired by the churches Bocabella had seen on a trip to Italy. The "Sagrada Familia" was to be built and maintained with donations only and without financial support from the bishopric. The project was entrusted to the diocesan architect Francisco del Villar, and the cornerstone was laid on St. Joseph's Day in 1882. The construction site was in "Ensanche," the "New City" of Barcelona, at the foot of Montaña Pelada and near the Gran Via Diagonal. Villar's plans, imitative of traditional styles and compatible with contemporary taste, called for a conventional placement of the structure in the monotonous, quadrilateral pattern of the streets in the Ensanche section. But just one year after construction had begun, serious disagreements between Villar and the administration led to his resignation. Bocabella proposed his technical advisor and the supervisor of the entire construction project, Juan Martorell, as Villar's successor; but the latter refused to accept in view of the delicate circumstances. Instead, he recommended his young assistant, the 31-year-old Gaudí, for this monumental task. Martorell considered Gaudí the only person adequately qualified for the job, and though Bocabella had confidence in the elegant young man's competence, he was unhappy about his lack of religious interest. Still, Bocabella granted Gaudí his elitist demand of complete artistic independence, and Gaudí assumed management of the construction site on November 3, 1883. In the course of the 43 years that Gaudí worked on the "Holy Temple," what was originally a purely professional interest turned into a profound devotion to this project, a devotion that blended religion and art together into a grand conception. We do not know exactly when this "high-living dandy" became an architect devoted solely to the service of God. But his pursuit of artistic perfection and absoluteness must have led him inexorably toward God, whom he referred to as "the great Master Builder."

133

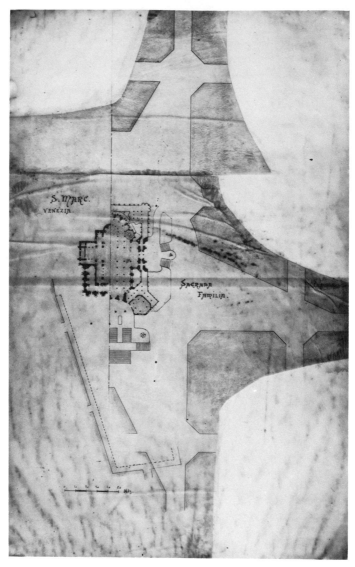

77   La Sagrada Familia. Plan of the grounds

78   La Sagrada Familia. Interior of the east façade during construction

It goes without saying that Gaudí could not accept either Villar's plans or the views of the authorities. He wanted to break up the monotony of the Ensanche section and place the building at a diagonal to the avenue that now bears his name (Fig. 77). So placed, the spires of this bulwark of the Catholic faith would have been a point of reference for the entire city, a symbol of the Christianization of restless Barcelona. The crypt shows little of Gaudí's architectural influence and remains a work of classical Gothic architecture from both a structural and an esthetic point of view. Gaudí was obliged to use the already existing clustered pillars, which set the main accent; but he heightened the vaults and transformed the dull character of the crypt by surrounding it with a kind of moat and substituting large windows for the porthole-like openings originally planned. The first mass was celebrated in 1891.

In the apse, Gaudí completely discarded Villar's neo-Gothic plan (Figs. 78, 79). Gaudí's options were limited in the sense that the foundations had already been laid, but in the use he made of them his totally personal interpretation of the principles of Gothic church construction come into play. In Gaudí's opinion, the problem of deflecting

135

79 La Sagrada Familia. Interior of the east façade after completion

80 La Sagrada Familia. East façade and apse ▷

81 La Sagrada
Familia. Interior
view of the east
façade and the
apse

the vault pressure had not been satisfactorily solved, and he condemned the flying buttress as an unimaginative makeshift. The buttress system, which verticalized the pressure and guided it through the supporting elements, is circumvented here by strengthening the load-bearing elements and walls and by lowering the height of the building. The outside view of the still unfinished apse makes the difference between it and the crypt obvious. The smooth, cold stone has given way to a lively surface texture; floral motifs smooth the harsh transitions and crown the six spires; the medieval animal symbols are modeled "naturally." The traditional Gothic shape of the windows has been replaced by arches and circles combined in non-prescribed ways (Fig. 80).

In 1895, once the crypt and the apse had been completed, Gaudí began designing the east façade. This move drew violent criticism at first because the west façade, which faced the city, had greater public exposure and therefore seemed a more urgent project. But Gaudí stuck to his plans for thematic reasons: The theme of the east façade was Christ's birth; and, in keeping with the actual sequence of events in the Savior's life, it had to come before the Passion, which was the theme of the west façade. Then, too, the side facing toward the sunrise symbolically proclaimed Christ's birth. The façade rests on four rectangular, diagonally placed towers which are arranged in pairs and provide niches for the figures. This configuration allows room for one main portal and two side portals.

Archivolts topped with lanterns rise from the diagonals of the portal entries. The façade consists of overlapping triangles on which naturalistic ornamentation is superimposed. The interior of the façade, dominated by simple geometric shapes, stands in contrast to the maelstrom of form on the exterior (Figs. 81, 82). The triptych is framed in by two lanterns, above which the bell towers rise. The columns, which resemble palm trees in conception, rest on the backs of turtles. The decorative figures portray episodes from the life of Jesus, and the portals embody the themes of faith, hope, and charity.

The portal of charity is divided by a pillar of bundled palm fronds. The base of this column is wreathed by natural forms artfully woven in wrought iron. The severity of the diagonal members is broken by horizontal stone corbels lavishly decorated with vegetable and zoo-

◁ 82   La Sagrada Familia. Interior view of the east façade

83   La Sagrada Familia. Gable of the east portal

84   La Sagrada Familia. Cross on the east portal ▷

morphic motifs. Sculptural ornamentation in the form of statues of Joseph, Mary, Jesus, and music-making angels (Fig. 85) is distributed over the entire portal and ties in with the rest of the decorative elements. Gaudí made his first sculptures for the façade—three versions of an angel—working from photographs of a live model. The realistically conceived figures are linked together by the simple abstract shapes of structurally functional supporting members that have a three-dimensional effect of their own. Out of the gable— the crowning glory of this portal—grows a green cypress with white doves, symbolizing purity, in its branches (Figs. 83, 84). Originally, Gaudí had planned to frame the sculptures in color. Dark blue, white, and silver were to predominate.

The flight into Egypt, shown in a fantastically conceived landscape, and the massacre of the children in Bethlehem are depicted in the portal of hope. Above these agitated scenes stands an allegorical representation of the holy mountain of Montserrat. Green, the color of hope, was planned as the dominant color.

The portal of faith displays figures of the young Jesus as a preacher and of Saint Elizabeth, Zachary, Joseph, and Mary (Fig. 87). Yellow and sienna were planned as the major colors here; the luxuriant plant ornamentation was to appear in natural colors.

Normally, cloisters are located on the side or the front of churches, but Gaudí chose to surround his church with a cloister-like structure to reduce the noise coming from the street. This cloister consists of cross vaults culminating in gables and dotted with rose windows. However, only two vault bays, on the sides of the east portal, were completed (Fig. 80). The entrance portal is dedicated to Our Lady of the Rosary, and the decorative shapes are derived from this theme (Fig. 88).

The four 100-meter [328 foot] high towers of the east façade are the last structures completed under Gaudí's direction. With a turn of remarkable ingenuity, he converted the originally rectangular pillars into round towers. With the help of a gallery he terminated the rectangular form and concealed the transitional point behind four 14-meter [46 foot] high figures of the apostles. The spiral structure of the towers with spiral staircases inside is modeled on a rotating parabola (Fig. 91). The simple effect of the structure is achieved, paradoxically enough,

◁ 85   La Sagrada Familia. East façade, detail with angels blowing trumpets

87   La Sagrada Familia. Portal of faith on the east side

◁ 86   La Sagrada Familia. Pinnacle of a tower on the east portal

by means of a complicated combination of forms: above a set of windows divided by sturdy columns and arranged spirally, we find a section of solid masonry work with the repeated inscription "Sanctus Sanctus" extending around it. Farther up, the paraboloid structure of the towers is executed in vertical stone shafts with horizontal members like the slanted slots of a blind between them (Fig. 92). The shape and cross section of the towers at any point is determined by the height.

The spires of the towers were not completed until after Gaudí's death. Designed to be viewed from a distance, they look like gigantic abstract sculptures in the shape of a bishop's miter, and they act as a visual counterweight to the sculptured ornamentation of the portals (Fig. 86). The spires rise from a truncated cone with a triangular base. Next comes a complicated system of pyramids, polygons, and rhombi that ends in two squares (back to back, and with curved sides). These squares, framed by spheres of various sizes, stand upright on one corner and are transected by a floral cross. Venetian glass, glazed tiles, and colored stones form a brilliant surface on which "Hosanna" and "Excelsis" are inscribed several times.

In 1917, Gaudí completed his sketch for the west façade. The theme of the west portal was Christ's Passion. The façade has a triangular base and is pyramidal in shape. Each side of the pyramid is made up of three inclined columns, and the entire structure forms a kind of shrine. The extremely attenuated pyramid evolves into a helicoid at its tip and forms a transition to the towers. A fish, the symbol of Christ, was planned for the top. The figures here, in contrast to the east portal, were to be kept at a minimum, thus lending emphasis to the figure of Christ on the cross, located on the doorpost (Fig. 94).

In Gaudí's plan, the southern front, with its main portal depicting the Last Judgment, was to dominate the exterior (Fig. 93); and he envisioned a 20-meter [65.6 foot] high portico leading to a representation of man in his eternal struggle for redemption. Gaudí had also planned to build a fountain and a beacon in front of the façade as symbols of purification. Four 100-meter [328 foot] high bell towers were planned for each façade. Taken together, they were to represent the twelve apostles.

88   La Sagrada Familia. Portal of Our Lady of the Rosary in the cloister   ▷

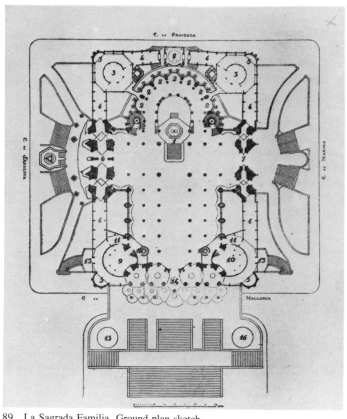

89 La Sagrada Familia. Ground plan sketch

90 La Sagrada Familia. Final transverse section drawing ▷

91 La Sagrada Familia. Descending spiral stairway in a tower ▷▷

92 La Sagrada Familia. Overhead view in a bell tower ▷▷

150

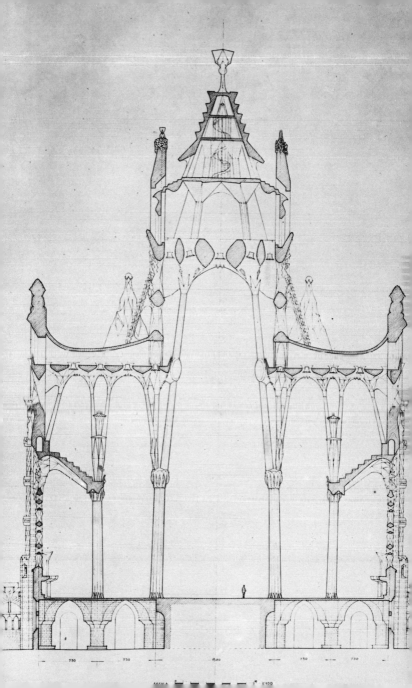

For the floor plan, Gaudí selected the traditional arrangement of a cross-shaped basilica. His plan called for a nave with four side aisles, a transept with two side aisles, an apse, and a foyer. He also wanted to include two baptistries and two sacristies between the apse and the cloister (Fig. 89).

In the construction of the Sagrada Familia, Gaudí employed new design principles, such as inclined, tree-like columns, and brought the use of curved surfaces to perfection. He thus liberated the Gothic pillar system from its disadvantages. He eliminated flying buttresses by using inclined columns that absorb both weight and thrust. The load-bearing supports of the Sagrada Familia are on the inside and remind us of trees not only in appearance but also in function because they bear loads that are independent of each other: at given heights, they divide into branches, and each branch rises toward the center of gravity of the particular vault section it is supposed to support (Fig. 90). The branches first absorb the load of each roof section and then carry it down to the main columns. Each of these hyperboloid or hyperbolic

93   La Sagrada Familia. Gaudí's conception of the completed church

154

94　La Sagrada Familia. Study for the west portal

paraboloid vault sections is reinforced with steel rods. The minor horizontal thrust in the vault is easily absorbed by the reinforcements.

Gaudí's choice of curved surfaces was dictated by economic as well as esthetic considerations. They were easy for the masons to build, and the straight steel rod reinforcements made them reasonable in terms of materials. In many respects, Gaudí's light shell vaults of brick over which concrete was poured anticipated the reinforced concrete shells of our day.

Gaudí lived to see only one of the four towers on the east façade completed—the southernmost one, dedicated to St. Barnabas. After his death, the three remaining towers were built under the direction of his collaborator Sugrañes who followed the original models and plans exactly (Fig. 78). Work on the east portals was completed in 1935; but Sugrañes' plan to build the sacristies was cut off abruptly by the Civil

War, in which Sugrañes was later killed in action. Construction of the "Temple" was not resumed until 1952, and at the time of this writing, the west façade is nearing completion.

It was Gaudí's wish that the interior of the Sagrada Familia be illuminated at night so that light would pour out through the perforated masonry. The building would then stand as a manifestation in stone of Christ's words: "I am the Light of the World!" (Fig. 95).

95   La Sagrada Familia. View of the east façade, illuminated from within   ▷

In Lieu of an Epilogue

Deprived of fixed points to orient himself by, of familiar landmarks, and of the experience of moving in a shaped environment, man becomes autistic in his emotional life and can relate only to himself. He will achieve only minimal levels of socialization, or may even become altogether asocial. The withdrawal of interest from ''objects'' that we can observe in so many people results to a considerable extent from the monotony of their existence, and this monotony derives in turn from the monotonous ugliness of the industrialized landscape in which they live, work, and seek amusement. In other words, their entire environment contributes to that monotony. . . . Our sense of home, of homeland, is rooted in a basic biological fact of life, and that fact is that every living creature needs a certain territory for its development.

Alexander Mitscherlich, *Thesen zur Stadt der Zukunft* [Theses on the city of the future]. Frankfurt am Main: Suhrkamp, 1971.

Appendix

Works

1895	Project for the Güell family tomb, Montserrat
1898–1900	Casa Calvet, Calle de Caspe 48, Barcelona
1898–1916	Chapel for the Güell workers' settlement, Santa Coloma de Cervelló
1900–02	Villa "Bellesguard," Calle de Bellesguard 16, Barcelona
1900–14	Park Güell, Barcelona
1900–16	"Mystery of the Rosary," sculptures, Montserrat
1901–02	Finca Miralles, wall and gates, Les Corts de Sarria, Barcelona
1902	Café Torino, interior decoration, Barcelona
1904	Sala Mercé, movie theater, Rambla, Barcelona
1904	House plans for the artist Luis Garner, Les Corts de Sarria, Barcelona
1904	Project for a bridge over the Pomeret River, Les Corts de Sarria, Barcelona
1904	Project for a warehouse for José Badia, Barcelona
1904–06	Casa Batlló, Paseo de Gracia, Barcelona
1904–14	Restoration of the Cathedral of Palma de Mallorca, Majorca
1906–08	Consultation on the restoration of the Barreo Gotico, Barcelona
1906–10	Casa Milá, Paseo de Gracia, Barcelona
1908	Project for a hotel in the United States
1908–10	Project for a chapel for the Colegio Teresiano, Barcelona
1909	School building of the Sagrada Familia, Barcelona
1910	Design for the monument to James I and design of the Plaza del Rey, Barcelona
1910	Street lights for the Plaza Mayor, Vich
1910	Exhibition of models, photographs, and drawings in the salon of the "Société Nationale des Beaux-Arts," Paris
1923	Studies for a chapel in Colonia Calvet, Torello

La Sagrada Familia

1882	Laying of the foundation stone
1882–1883	Work by Francisco del Villars
1883–91	Crypt
1891–92	Apse
1891–1900	East façade depicting the Nativity of Christ
1891–1900	Cloister and rose portal
1901–26	Towers and pinnacles
1911–17	West façade, the Passion
ca. 1916	South façade, Judgment Day
ca. 1925	Sacristies
1882–1926	Drawings, plans, models

160

Biographical Dates

1813–1906	Francisco Calderero, Antoni Gaudí's father
1843–1876	Antonia Cornet, Antoni Gaudí's mother
June 25, 1852	Antoni Gaudí y Corn'et born in Reus in the Province of Tarragona
1864	Enters the Instituto de Segunda Ensenanza in Reus
1869	Enrollment in the School of Science, University of Barcelona
1873	Enters the Escola Superior d'Architectura, Barcelona
1878	Final examinations
1879–ca. 1890	Membership in "Centre Excursionista Catalana"
1880	First meeting with Eusebio Güell
1887	Trip to North Africa
1887	Friendship with Bishop Juan Grau
1890	Begins intensive religious studies
1914–1926	Complete devotion to his principal work, the "Sagrada Familia"
1920	Arrested during political unrest
June 7, 1926	Gaudí is hit by a trolley car on the present Avenida de José Antonio
June 10, 1926	Antoni Gaudí y Corn'et dies in the Hospital of Santa Cruz in Barcelona
June 12, 1926	Funeral ceremony

Bibliography

Albanesi, Assunta. "Divagazioni su Antonio Gaudí: un tempio come base spaziale, architetto Enrico Castiglione." *L'Architettura*, September 1957, pp. 318–322.

Boada, J. Puig. *El Temple de la Sagrada Familia*. Barcelona: Ediciones Omega, 1952.

Bergós, Joan. *Antoni Gaudí, l'home i l'obra*. Barcelona: Ariel, 1954.

Casanelles, E. *Antonio Gaudí: A Reappraisal*. Greenwich, Connecticut: New York Graphic Society, 1967.

Cirlot, Juan Eduardo. *El Arte de Gaudí*. Barcelona: Ediciones Omega, 1950.

Collins, George R. *Antonio Gaudí*. New York: G. Braziller, 1960.

——————— . *Antonio Gaudí and the Catalan Movement*. Charlottesville: University Press of Virginia (American Society of Architectural Bibliographers), 1973.

Elias, Jorge. *Gaudí, assaig biografic*. Barcelona: Ediciones "Circo," 1961.

Folguera, Francisco. *L'Arquitectura Gaudíniana*. Barcelona: Editorial Canosa, 1929.

Hitchcock, Henry-Russell. *Gaudí*. New York: Museum of Modern Art, 1957.

Martinell, César. *Gaudí i la Sagrada Familia comentada per ell mateix*. Barcelona: Aymá, 1951.

——————— . *Gaudínismo*. Barcelona: "Amigos de Gaudí," 1952.

——————— . *Antonio Gaudí*. Milan: Electa, 1955.

—————— . *Gaudí: His Life, His Theories, His Work*. Translated from the Spanish by Judith Rohrer. Edited by George R. Collins. Cambridge, Massachusetts; MIT Press, 1975.

Nonell Bassegoda, Juan. *Gaudí*. Madrid: Publicaciones Españolas, 1971.

Pane, Roberto. *Antoni Gaudí*. Milan: Edizioni di Communità, 1964.

Pellicer, A. Cirici. *El arte modernista catalán*. Barcelona, 1951.

Prats Vallés, J. *Gaudí*. Barcelona: Editorial RM, 1958.

Ráfols, José. *Gaudí*. Barcelona: Editorial Canosa, 1929.

—————— . *Modernismo y modernistas*. Barcelona: Aymá, 1949.

Rubió Tuduri, Santiago. *Cálculo funicular del hormigón armado: Generalización de los métodos de cálculo y proyecto del arquitecto Gaudí a las estructuras del hormigón armado*. Buenos Aires: Ediciones G. Gili, 1952.

Sellés y Baró, Salvador. "El parque Güell." *Anuario de la Asociación de Arquitectos de Cataluña*, 1903, pp. 47–67.

Sert, José Luis. "A Pictorial Excursion into the Unique Gaudí World." *Progressive Architecture*, March 1959.

Sugrañes, Domingo. "Disposición estática del Templo de la Sagrada Familia." *Anuario de la Asociación de Arquitectos de Cataluña*, 1923, pp. 17–36.

Sweeney, James Johnson and José Luis Sert. *Antoni Gaudí*. New York: Praeger, 1961.

Tarragó Cid, Salvador. *Gaudí*. Paris: Imp. Tournon, 1971.

For a complete bibliography, including all of the articles on Gaudí in periodicals, see the above-mentioned work by George R. Collins for the American Society of Architectural Bibliographers, *Antonio Gaudí and the Catalan Movement*.

List of Illustrations

Photo Credits

Index

The italicized numbers refer to illustrations.

172

About the Author

Gabriele Sterner, born in 1946, studied art history, archeology, and philosophy in France and Italy. In 1970, she earned her Ph.D., writing her dissertation on French Art Nouveau under Professor Wolfgang Braunfels in Munich. She is a freelance consultant to the "Neue Sammlung" [New collection] and the Villa Stuck Museum in Munich and has organized numerous exhibitions: *Art Deco—Decoration and Books* (Munich, Hamburg, Berlin, and Pforzheim); *Photographic Views of Munich* (Munich); *Art Nouveau—Jugendstil—Modern Style* (for the Goethe Institute; Paris); *Christian Schad—Drawings and Woodcuts* (Munich). Among her publications are *Zinn vom Mittelalter bis zur Gegenwert* [Pewter from the Middle Ages to the present], *Fruhtrunk, Photoansichter von München* [Photographic views of Munich], and a number of magazine articles. Barron's has also published *Art Nouveau* by Gabriele Sterner.